Judaism and Tragic Theology

Judaism & Tragic Theology

Frederick S. Plotkin

Foreword by Arthur A. Cohen

SCHOCKEN BOOKS · NEW YORK

Library of Congress Catalog Card No. 73–81343
Manufactured in the United States

To My Beloved Wife,
Diana Shulamit

Contents

Foreword
by Arthur A. Cohen

Frederick Plotkin's JUDAISM AND TRAGIC THEOLOGY is that anomaly in the history of Jewish thought—a philosophy of religion. The anomalous character of the enterprise is less the fact of its rarity, even its uniqueness, than the conviction which motivates its composition. Why a philosophy of religion? Why even more a philosphy of religion loosely wooven from the strands of historical Jewish sources?

Philosophy of religion is in itself a curious discipline. It is an historical, even a literary, mode which has been undertaken and refined many times, more often by Platonists of Christian persuasion (or Christians of Platonic persuasion) to provide a link between the vision of the Gospels and the findings of metaphysics. I have read in earlier days—days when I, too, was embarrassed by the findings of faith—many philosophies of religion, hoping that they would supply me with the reasonable conditions which would enable the dramas of the religious life to be enacted with ruminative pipe in hand, cat at knee, and an unhurried heartbeat. Alas, philosophies of religion didn't work. They were finally defeated by the incommensurability of the subject-matter of the discipline and the caution of their method. At the same time as they were concerned to assert no more than their premises would allow they were so scrupulous in the definition of their premises that the object of the inquiry, the living God, all but disappeared into the categories of caution.

This general problem of the philosophic inquiry into religion is not restricted to the undertakings of Christian thinkers. It affects that of Jews as well, the most notable and pre-eminent being Hermann Cohen, whose *Religion of Reason Out of the Sources of Judaism* is an attempt to describe the nature and activity of God according to the sources and models of Jewish prophetic tradition. Cohen not unlike other philosophers of religion allows no more of God than he can rationally describe. God is a reality, but real only insofar as the mind and its operations are real, ethical only insofar as human enterprise demands ethical imperatives, salvific only insofar as history has an ethical intention. In other words, as the young *bachur* said to Cohen–reducing him to tears–he had demonstrated the God of philosophy from the sources of Judaism, but where was the *ribbono shel olam,* the Master of the World. The living God, living and · therefore indescribable, exceeding all categories, transcending any and every premise, carrying within himself all the energy not merely of general and abstract life but of life particular and concrete was lost in the machinery of the system. Philosophy of religion comes before God from the other side of divinity. Inescapably anthropocentric, God is a bodying-forth, an excursion of the mind

But if philosophy of religion makes God the deduction of reason, is theology any the less troubled? What is the difference between philosophy of religion and theology? For one thing philosophy of religion stands outside the circle of faith, whereas theology begins within it. Philosophy of religion can imagine that its considerations are general, that its inquiry is abstract, its methodology ratiocinative and experiential, its argumentation indifferent to the listings and ballast of the Holy Spirit (read historical divigation, for the Holy Spirit in action is always historical), but it is finally particular. The philosopher of religion is never as impartial as he pretends. He makes Christianity (or Judaism) reasonable, because he wants his religion, but he wants it plausible and unhysterical. He wants a general God, a viable morality, an acceptable ethos, but it is finally a Christian heaven (or the *yeshivah shel maalah*) to which he wants access.

All talk about God is finally historical and particular. There is no general god only the God of the Cross or the God of Abraham, Isaac, and Jacob. Theology, unlike philosophy of religion, Karl Barth unlike Pringle-Pattison, Franz Rosenzweig unlike Hermann Cohen, begins with the given, the datum of the Holy Word and works from there. Even Rosenzweig, the greatest Jewish thinker of our time, perhaps the greatest Jewish thinker in many centuries, works through a palimpsest of languages and styles, each echoing and re-echoing experiences whose progenitive authority is scriptural. Book One of *The Star of Redemption,* which invariably baffles and enrages those who pursue religion, like an exotic comestible is grounded upon Scripture; the elements of the universe, God, man, world, self-enclosed and self-generative and defining, nevertheless reflect the shadow of the hooded lights of Scripture, hooded lights focused directly in Book Two and revealed, naked and unshaded, in the last book. In other words, *The Star of Redemption,* unlike *The Religion of Reason,* is always argued from within the magic forest of the Word—the Word of God is always there, reverberating within the brain of Franz Rosenzweig, whereas for Hermann Cohen the task is to condition the ear that it can allow itself to hear (a metaphor which at least enables us to recognize the difference between theology and philosophy of religion, but not only a metaphor since it discloses something of the attitude which a man assumes when he comes to think about God).

JUDAISM AND TRAGIC THEOLOGY is related to philosophy of religion, but nonetheless manages to maintain its distance from the pretensions and ensnarements of a self-satisfied reason. The perspective is one of science and reason, the findings of linguistic analysis and depth psychology—indeed, the whole armamentarium of modern science—but it is still not philosophy of religion in the old sense in which we have used the term. Plotkin does not, as did Rudolph Otto in his own *Philosophy of Religion,* seek simply to document the rational content of religious belief (having satisfied his discovery of the nonrational content by his antecedent *The Idea of the Holy*). The predicament which Plotkin addresses is one founded upon the Heraclitean intuition of the flux—the thinker tries to position himself, but the ground under his feet, the sky above his head, the aether within his brain moves, endlessly moves. The thinker is then without fixed standpoint. He cannot regard any single methodology as complete and adequate, any system of reason as impregnable. His is no conventional philosophy of religion. He does not, as Hermann Cohen, begin by describing the content of science and the differentia between science and religion, specifying the dissimilarities of method and procedure. Cohen begins by telling us how he is going to think. Plotkin begins by putting us right before the issue as he conceives it. His philosophy of religion—of Jewish religion most particularly, Jewish religion in tension with Jewish secularism—begins with adumbrations of the precarious condition of man, man the creature who sins and dies, perhaps who dies because he sins (a not uncurious argument). The reality of evil and death is the background of his reflections, and in this he joins those many existential thinkers of our time who consider the prospect of death and the afflictions of evil to be the ultimate sources of man's quest for meaning.

I have come to think, although without the machinery of Freud's empirical method, that besides the pleasure principle, man pursues self-justification. If the pleasure principle reflects libidinal urgency, primal to the strivings of men, and indeed not unrelated to the bodings of theodicy, the quest for self-vindication, a quest which quickens in man's middle years and reaches its fullest measure of anguish and centrality toward the close of life, is its companion. Freud is only too aware that the desire for pleasure and the minimalization of pain is never adequately realized—censored by the superego, trampled by convention, suppressed, deflected, and displaced by the requirements of civilization, man's energy for pleasure is continuously challenged by the claim of the other (the other as superego, parent, culture, civilization) that not pleasure, but work and utility, is the acceptable course for men. Surrounding, then, the quest for satiety of passions is the early implantation of mechanisms of restraint and control. It is only later, much later, when the restraints have been felt as punishments and the controls as deprivations, that the pains and sufferings of existence become obtrusive. Contained too often by fear, fettered not infrequently by guilt and anxiety, men pass by the offerings of reality—their unique chance—and later in the hours of retrospection the question not simply of justice but of justification looms large. Every man, whatever his condition or experience, tests the product of his life against its possibility and finds it wanting. It is, at those moments, that he renews either the procedures of self-punition or undertakes the last heroism which is to objectify like Koheleth the procedures of the world, to acknowledge that as it is to him so is it to all men, that all life seeks its goal and failing it, either deepens the inculpation and despair or recognizes that such is the course of life.

The philosophy of religion, that rational propaedeutic to belief and religious practice, is an intermediate medicament to the despair which dogs our pursuit of justification. Traditional and familiar philosophies of religion begin with a somewhat hard-headed presupposition that nothing will be said of the religious sense in man or the religious object in the universe unless it can be demonstrated as having at least possible confirmation in the experiences and reflections of intelligent men. In other words, reason will supply the grounding and conditions of intelligent belief, recognizing of course—as thinkers beyond the age of Kierkergaard have been obliged to recognize—that there is still a difference between belief and faith. But such a procedure, however it may work for the Christian philosopher of religion, does not work for the Jew. The Jewish thinker cannot as the Christian argue up to the borders of faith and then turn man over to grace to conduct him further into the interior landscape of the religious life. The Jewish thinker, however far he may be, in personal observance, from the *halakhah,* still has a customary *praxis* lodged in his understanding of religion. The measure of the Jew is not the quality of his faithfulness, but his witness and exemplification. One does not become a *tzaddik* by right belief, but only by the example of practice. Plotkin is very much aware of this, and it is his unargued recognition of the chasm which separates Judaism and Christianity (and leaves his book remarkably unpolemical, undefensive, and unapologetic before Christianity—in itself a noteworthy achievement) which turns his investigation into a new and fresh direction. Plotkin is clearly a believer, not an arguer to his own belief. He stands within the circle of belief and practice. Why then the urgency to make philosophy of religion? It is his conviction that the situation of Judaism as a world religion is precarious, that Judaism as religion is intrinsically valuable, that its vision is realistic and true, that its response to the inquiries of men is, however its internal incapsulation and historic unwillingness to join the issue with the non-Jewish (hence unenlightened) world, profound and viable. Plotkin's concern is not that Judaism needs defense or explication, but rather that the sovereignty of its truth withers from neglect and desuetude, that Jews leave Judaism (however much they may retain their espousal as Jews–culturalists, nationalists, secular Messianists) because they are unable to square the biblical and halakhic vision of the world with the intellectual requirements of modernity. The argument then of JUDAISM AND TRAGIC THEOLOGY is mediated through the search for a viable system of translation, a new language which will enable the ancient scriptural perception of man, history, and God to be articulated in the conceptual formulations of science, linguistics, phenomenology, and depth psychology. His undertaking, profound as it is, is pursued with splendid modesty, trenchantly argued, humanely exemplified, it is nonetheless marked by a spirit of graceful sensitivity to the difficulties which adhere to his method. Since he stands within the circle of faith and looks out over its circumference to the *terra incognita* of scientific demurral, he cannot be too harsh in dogmatizing his own certainties. He is a modern man and a believing Jew; he knows the intellectual disciplines through which the grammar of mediation is pursued and yet he has the sureness of a man of faith. In other words there is a real sense in which his philosophy of religion is not the attempt to describe the possibilities of belief to reason or to discover the warrant for what sentiment has already predisposed him to cherish. He is trying something more daring, which is to make his life as a believing Jew intelligible to his intellect. Although he guards against the incursions of subjectivity, he cannot eliminate them. He walks the tightrope and he walks it well.

The difficulty of his argument is that he tries to accomplish too much. The breadth of his knowledge, his familiarity with the literatures grown up during recent decades to redefine the understanding of language, philosophy, social anthropology, and sociology of knowledge frequently strain his attention to his principal insight which derives from his conception of the tragic displacement of man before God. I would have wished that he might have pressed that argument further before moving on. As it is I can only express the doubt proposed by Baruch Kurzweil in his splendid essay "Job and the Possibility of Biblical Tragedy"* that there is no such thing as tragedy in the Bible; indeed, how could there be if the relation between man and God is absolute? But then the appropriate counter might well be that such a denial of tragedy to biblical man rests more on an acceptance of the criteria prescribed by Aristotle's Poetics for the structure of tragedy, that the tragic hero is not destroyed by gods but by his peers and the fatality which moves through them. Plotkin's response would most certainly be that the Bible does not contain tragedy, but that all men, no less the men of Scripture, are tragic. The human condition, he would insist, is tragic whereas I could say the human condition is real and reality is not tragic, only difficult.

Be these cavils as they may, JUDAISM AND TRAGIC THEOLOGY is an original, profound, wide-ranging, always suggestive introduction to the consideration of fundamental questions of religious epistemology, method, and teaching from the sources of science and historic Judaism. It will displease those who would have wanted a more traumatic dramatization of Jewish conscience, a more stressful forcing of the consequence of the Holocaust (which is only mentioned in passing), a more urgent apostrophizing of the decision for Judaism and Jewish identity, but such displeasure would really miss the point. Plotkin is not unaware of the crisis in Jewish identity, but he has chosen a more patient and intellectually honest approach than that of knocking Jewish sense into Jewish heads. He is doing the more seductive, but also the more dangerous and enduring work of trying to persuade, of making cogent and reasonable the intuitions of historical Judaism. The intelligence

*Arthur A. Cohen, *Arguments and Doctrines, a Reader of Jewish Thinking in the Aftermath of the Holocaust* (New York: Harper & Row, 1970), pp. 323–344.

of the uncommitted must first be swerved out of its pitted and routinized paths before it can be religiously formed and instructed. That preliminary undertaking has been splendidly and suggestively explored in JUDAISM AND TRAGIC THEOLOGY and the book itself should make its method especially attractive in the teaching of Jewish religion in the light of modern science and the modern sensibility.

May 13, 1973

Judaism and Tragic Theology

Introduction

All men are sinners and all men must die. Judaism takes these facts in bitter earnest and can certainly never endorse facile phrases about evil somehow being good. A faith born in the shadow of the Golden Calf knows too much about tragedy for that. What, after all, can be more appalling than the fact that a man can destroy his own soul, spread corruption into the souls around him, and perhaps bring ruin upon a generation? To call such calamities somehow good is utter nonsense. Nor is it in the least a "Jewish" sentiment to pretend to ourselves that evil or death "do not matter." It is thought to be "religious" to talk like that; but it is a false and hollow sentimentalism and it is, to my mind, shockingly un-Jewish. What can be more awful to contemplate than the prospect of spiritual torment or of bodily dissolution? What can seem a more complete denial of life and love than the corpse of someone dear to us? Death is the annihilation of everything. If anyone tells me that mortality does not matter and that as a Jew I must not mind too much, he simply does not know what he is talking about. I do not believe that true Jewish thinking will ever attempt to minimize the horror of it.

There are, however, two attitudes which may (and perhaps should) be cultivated, which will involve a certain measure of discipline and detachment from currently "fashionable" deterministic and fatalistic outlooks on man's tragic condition and Judaism's tragic sense of life. The first is a readiness to bear the limitations and trials of our Jewish existence, which is human existence, as part of our creaturehood and submission to the will of God. This can be a real sacrifice, or even a real covenant act of *hesed* (righteousness), and not merely something put up with. Delimitation of self runs counter to a common modern Jewish assumption that all deprivation or pain is somebody's fault, or due to unwillingness in others or in society to ameliorate our lot.

Jews know that pain, suffering, loss, intellectual confusion, emotional confusion, and disappointment are inherent in our mortal and imperfect world: "Man is born to trouble as the sparks fly upward" (Job 5:7). This insight does not oppose all that skill and legislation can do to relieve human distress; rather, the *aperçu* is a witness to the truth that, when everything of this sort is done, or at the very least attempted, Jews are still left with menace and frustration—because Jews remain spirit-centered beings.

To come to terms with the limits of self, demands both a recovery of inner freedom and a way of devotion and giving (*tzedakah*), in a world which grows bitter and resentful at the slightest misery. And, indeed, it is likely that when men are relieved by applied science from the struggle for livelihood and by welfare measures from social insecurity, which have absorbed so much attention in the past, the deeper problems of personal existence will loom even larger as the sphere of trouble. It would be calamitous if the Jewish community were not able to respond to this residue of the human struggle with its inevitable perplexities, frustrations, and anxieties, when the illusion is dispelled that knowledge and government can root out all dissatisfactions.

The second general attitude which, I am suggesting, requires cultivation is respect for what is given to Jews in this generation. This includes the earth's life, which provides the basis of what the scientific community can erect out of it, and also the inheritance of the past. The present generation does not lack admiration for men's intellectual powers, it does, however, suffer from what Bertrand Russell has called "cosmic impiety" and from irreverence toward what former ages have bequeathed to us.

The modern Jew does not reverence the created world the more for having ceased to reverence God and Torah. He is mainly stirred by what can be done to the given world and by what can be done to create the future. The givenness of things, the bases of life in families, traditions, institutions, histories—things that have grown and are not manufactured, what is delivered to us through the five bodily senses and our share in the cultural inheritance—these things which were formerly snares to sensuality or lethargy have now become a foreign realm overshadowed by man's technical and organizational abilities to manipulate his environment. Further, the proliferation of information via the new visual media gives to the young, and the not so young, many more indirect and secondhand mental pictures of realities which they do not touch, contemplate, share in, or have to come to terms with.

People now obtain vast amounts of surrogate knowledge *about* facts which they do not directly experience. Overcoming the pull of the world today clearly involves a certain withdrawal from this secondhand mental world in order to encounter what is given by the natural order and through our cultural and historical inheritance. Such a withdrawal would be in some ways a reversal of traditional ascetic practices of historical Judaism, but something of the kind is demanded, it seems to me, by the situation in which men's contact with things has been overlaid by their desire to fabricate technically and mentally an artificial second nature. It is this cerebralized, secularized, and technologically super-sacramentalized world which I am suggesting should be renounced by means of a new kind of ascesis, not in order to escape from our responsibilities to the Secular City, but in order that it shall not completely envelop our souls.

In most Jewish circles today, it is a commonplace that it is possible to speak of God only because God has spoken of himself. We have knowledge of him, a contemporary argument runs, through the instrument of our biblical or "natural" religion, which expresses God's revelatory word through nature in what we have become accustomed to term a pure state, i.e., not as mere elaborations or as attributes. Furthermore, it is said that Jews believe that they have knowledge of God as he manifests himself to man in progressive stages of creation and unfolding through his image, which is called his spirit, and through his prophets. Yet despite our occasionally collective syncretist sense that our religious faith of Judaism is a mere phase in the history of religions, an incomplete and even, perhaps, inadequate experience of God which only partially witnesses a single and idiosyncratic form of the "transcendental unity" of all religion, it is good from time to time to take comfort from the thought that Judaism is not merely a manifestation of an immanent evolution of the religious genius of mankind, of which *my* particular faith may simply be a relatively higher expression; for if religious faith manifests anything at all, it is the fact of the intervention in human history of a transcendent God who introduces all of us into a domain which is radically closed to man in general. But it must be confessed that our religion and our commitment to a certain quality of life that acknowledges a source beyond itself is not the same thing at all as the idea that this source, or this "Other," is unfolding to us that which otherwise would be hidden, whether or not we choose to attribute to this source predicatives, attributes, or traits of the divine. Indeed, in this sense Jewish faith may be justifiably opposed to revelation.

Today, when it is so common to hear so many fundamental questions raised, which within the milieu of both our religion and our encompassing society provoke lively debate and even deep division—questions such as "Yet God is silent?" or "Are not the horizons of our religion shrouded in impenetrable gloom?"—the genuine secularists are recognizable by their having moved far beyond what they believe to be merely "dialogist" questions asked by religious men of other religions; the Jewish secularists contend that the very posing of such questions obliges the questioner to stand in some sort of proprioceptive and balanced relationship with the beliefs of all religions. Indeed they assert that the asking of such questions is the inevitable consequence of vain endeavors on the part of men of religious faith to bring the beliefs of religion into more or less agreeable harmony with various modern conceptions of the natural world. In short, they argue that to ponder these imponderables is to become an apologist for religion, which, in their sense of the term, includes all those who are still within the sphere of influence of any sort of belief in transcendent and supra-sensory realities, whether the belief be traditionally biblical, halakhic, idealistic, anthroposophical, communitive, or mystical in form.

Jewish secularists, then, demand that men of faith treat them with unusual consideration because they are, apart from matters of belief, men exemplary in all things. It is, moreover, characteristic of the genuine secularist that events in the world do not seem in the least obscure or problematic to him, but perfectly clear and intelligible. He is not only serene but silent; accusations against divine order or revelation are not uttered at all. With the collapse of what he feels to be naïve, providential concepts of order, all complaints against the ordering of the world and all questions concerning the reasons for it have lost their meaning for him; and, unlike the circus hand who drugs his lions before entering the cage, the Jewish secularist in our midst chooses to hunt what he understands to be the wild beast of concrete, social reality in the jungle where it lives.

In short, the secularist proposition that the study of the "social realities" of religion is the key to understanding the relationship of man to society is a concept gaining more credibility; for if religion, as they argue, is defined in functional terms, then Judaism of all the religions is perhaps the most significant to those compound systems of meaning and expression that permit man to transcend his own limits. Today, not unlike Robinson Crusoe, individual Jews who have become accustomed to function in isolation around separate and autonomous poles of subjective processes and precarious private systems have increasingly come to feel that they can assure "selfhood" only by traversing a communal path whose end is the construction of an objective, moral universe of meaning. Indeed, it has become virtually a commonplace in contemporary Jewish America that by this means—a process of building the self and society in relation to shared world-views—sacred meaning is revealed to man.

They assert that this process has been historically normative in Western religions; true enough, but it should be acknowledged that the symbol systems of most religions—and the corresponding structural embodiments of these symbols—have taken many different forms historically: institutional denominationalism, religious organizations, particular texts, doctrines, rituals, and so on. In our contemporary Jewish milieu, therefore, when such historically "official" models have visibly deteriorated, or more properly seem to have been frozen into immobile forms so that they can no longer cope either with a literate, mobile society under rapidly changing conditions or with the contextually religious problems and issues of selfhood and society, religion and religiosity have, indeed, appeared in novel, disguised, and often unexpected forms. But if modern Judaism has generated new religious beliefs and structures, it must be recognized that these new forms are often invisible because most of us have been trained and conditioned to perceive and respond to traditional forms.

Since Martin Buber and Franz Rosenzweig, it has become customary in Jewish philosophical circles to speak of the personal and social sources of denominationalism; but now the Jewish secularist is making it not only possible, but necessary, for the rest of Judaism to speak of the social sources of nondenominationalism as well, i.e., the explicit and intense relationship that has developed between the increasing socialization of modern man and the decreasing internalization by the modern Jew of the traditionally sacred models of his society. Simply to recognize the increasing secularization of modern American Jewry is not enough, for the problems of ultimate meaning remain.

Ultimate meanings notwithstanding, this much may be observed about "nondenominationalism" in this specialized, social world of contemporary Jewish America that is fundamentally different from anything our faith has experienced before: assortments and groupings of heterodox ideas and concepts have been fashioned by our rabbis, laymen, and intellectual spokesmen alike into precarious subjective systems which herald multiple, ultimate significances. As subjectively oriented social systems, each with its functional and autonomous rationality, each tends to reinforce man's sense of isolation from his milieu and each interacts with the new, commonly held "sacred idea"—the absolute autonomy of the individual. Furthermore, many of the new religious forms are characterized by a nearly total absence of traditional obligations of Judaism, i.e., belief in the divinity of either God or the natural world is gratuitous and entirely voluntary; but while the new forms support, hasten, and radicalize the depersonalization of society, they also "sanctify" by ritual fictions and acts the liberation of man's consciousness from the strictures and constraints of the social structure. Before any final judgments are made of the long-range effects on Judaism of these new forms, it would perhaps be well to examine with more care the effects upon the individual Jew; to "depersonalize" the Jew in twentieth-century America may result in a condition of virtually absolute human freedom; and then again, it may once more cast him into another wilderness and leave him to wander alone without compass, adrift in the desert. For the committed Jew, today, as it has always been with his ancestors, only time will tell.

During the greater part of the religious history of Judaism, union with God implied efforts to overcome the pull of nature, the egoisms of power and place, or the narcotic effects of social conformity. Now the main tentacles which imprison our souls embrace not only the products of man's mental powers, chiefly our technical and commercial civilization and the bewildering intellectual equipment required to live in it; they also include disorders of overwrought feelings, anxieties about one's inner state, confusions caused by the interaction of traditional ethical values of Torah Judaism with superannuated hypotheses of modern science, difficulties of choosing the "right" prophylactics offered by medicine, psychology, social theory, and new religious cults.

This outer and inner world of modern culture is so full of problems that it draws the human spirit to concentrate upon it, like the aching tooth drawing the tongue to itself. It is therefore urged that a new ascetic be developed by means of which the human spirit can regain its freedom from the domination of this secondary reality. This is not to be understood as a new Jewish heterodoxy, despising man's mastery over nature and the means of life. There is no Prometheus myth in Torah; but there is the expulsion from Eden, the Tower of Babel, the story of Job, and the prophetic books, all of which say that unless God's creatures, however spiritually powerful, recognize their creaturely limitations, there will be chaos without and within.

It is from within the frame of reference suggested by these two general attitudes I have described that I have attempted in this volume to counteract, in some small measure, the influence of our contemporary society and intellectual milieu upon Judaism, an influence which hinders faith more by drawing men's purposeful and emotional life to themselves than by intellectual movements of unbelief. It is all very well to say that Jews can get what they want from prayer, from history, from modern philosophy, psychology, and communications theory, etc., and still remain Jews; but when a habit is formed of unquestioning submission to the often contradictory demands of modernity, or to whatever comes along, the more difficult it is to read, listen, and evaluate responsibly.

The whole impact of these things encourages a blotting-paper, passive attitude to what impinges on the mind. When the values of Judaism cease to be "translated" in a coherent way into contemporary idioms, accessible to the linguistic, logical, and critical demands of "new" languages (i.e., phenomenology, sociology, perception, logical positivism, relativism, biology, and so forth), the Jew is obliged, even compelled, to accept a pattern of thought where he becomes egregiously engaged in private receptivity; the inner life of a Jew in the modern world is fissiparated, and his social intercourse destroyed.

1

Judaism and Tragic Theology

Where God is perceived as the origin of justice and the source of legislation, the problem of just sanctions is raised with an unprecedented seriousness; suffering emerges as an enigma when the demands of justice can no longer explain it; this enigma is the product of ethical theology itself. That is why the virulence of the book of Job is without equivalent in any culture; Job's complaint supposes the full maturity of an ethical vision of God; the clearer God becomes as legislator, the more obscure he becomes as creator; the irrationality of power balances the ethical rationalization of holiness; it becomes possible to turn the accusation back against God, against the ethical God of the accusation. Thereupon begins the dubious business of trying to justify God: theodicy (and its counterpart, anthropodicy) is born.

At this point of doubt, when the spontaneous ethical vision appeals to the arguments of theodicy and has recourse to a rhetoric of conviction, the possibility of a tragic vision looms up. That possibility is born of the impossibility of saving the ethical vision with the aid of any "proof." The friends of Job do indeed mobilize forgotten sins, unknown sins, ancestral sins, the sins of the people, in order to restore the equation of suffering and punishment; but Job refuses to close the gap. His innocence and his suffering are marginal to any ethical vision. Job is the personage who serves as touchstone for the ethical vision of the world and makes it fly to pieces.

By hypothesis or by construction, Job is innocent; he must be in order that the problem be posed in all its intensity: How is it possible that a man so wholly just should be so totally suffering? How does it come about that the imaginings of the extremes of the just and the unjust are enveloped in the representation of gradual guilt? To paraphrase Roland Barthes, Job is the zero degree of guilt joined to the extreme of suffering; from this conjunction is born the scandal which also is extreme.

This concern with the turn from ethical comprehension to tragic comprehension of God himself is the subject, direct and indirect, of all Jews who are alive to the possibilities of recovering the hyperethical dimension of God; one may argue from this context that to turn the alleged justice of the law of retribution against God is to make God appear "unjustifiable" from the point of view of the scheme of justification that had guided the whole process of "ethicization" of the Divine in biblical Israel. Hence one may be led to emphasize the tone of legal pleading in the book of Job, which turns against the earlier theodicy invoked by the three "friends" (Job 13:2–3, 15).

Is it not the tragic God that Job discovers (Job 7:8), the inscrutable God of terror? Tragic, too, is the denouement. "Suffering for the purpose of understanding," the Greek chorus said. Job, in his turn, penetrates beyond any ethical vision to a new dimension of unverifiable faith. What remains before the reader, however, is the fact of Job's plaint; even when Job seems to be destroying the basis of any dialogical relation between God and man, Job does not cease to move in the field of invocation, for it is to God that Job appeals against God (Job 14:13–14). Yet this is a faith that gets its veracity from the very defiance that argues against the vain science of retribution and renounces the wisdom that is inaccessible to man; when the God who answers Job "out of the whirlwind" reverses the relation of questioner and questioned and obliges Job to speak, Job returns to the crushing silence of resignation.

For those who read Job's silence ironically as a seal of his reconciliation to a God who does not hold out carrots on a stick for little donkeys to follow, Job's silence might be undersood as a kind of quietus on magic. God's distance from man is here maintained in such a reading, for man cannot control God by being good. But his nearness is also maintained, for Yahweh came to speak to Job, not with the intention of smashing him shuddering to the ground but in order to draw him back to himself. This reading stands midway between a view which holds Job's silence to be not altogether the seal of meaninglessness and one which asserts that it represents the zero degree of speech.

Certain words are addressed to Job in exchange for his silence, this special argument runs. These words are not an answer to his problem, however; they are not at all a solution to the problem of suffering; they are in no way a reconstruction, at a higher degree of subtlety, of the ethical vision of Judaism.

The God to whom Job is reconciled is not bound to man's ideas of him; God is not required to come at the snap of the good man's moral fingers. The God who addresses Job out of the tempest shows him Leviathan and Behemoth, the hippopotamus and the crocodile, all vestiges of the chaos that has been overcome, all representing a brutality dominated and measured by God's creative act. Through these symbols, he gives Job to understand that all is order, measure, and beauty—inscrutable order, measure beyond measure, terrible beauty. Such a reading enables one to mark out a way between agnosticism and the penal view of history and life—the way of a faith that reconciles man to God on God's terms, not on man's. God finds man guilty and acquits him—this is the fundamental irony of Job, and, to many Jews today, of all forms of biblical faith.

In this context, the author of Job, like Anaximander and Heraclitus the Obscure, may be seen to announce an order beyond order, a totality full of meaning, within which the individual must lay down his recrimination. Suffering cannot be explained, ethically or otherwise; but the contemplation of the whole initiates a movement which must be completed in a practical way by the surrender of the claim to form by oneself a little island of meaning in the universe. According to this view, the poet of Job, protesting a more profound search for "profit" by the use of the "magical" power of morality, proposes that the indicative is a living, personal faithfulness between man and God.

Carrying this argument somewhat further than its proponents would perhaps wish, one might ask: Of what can Job repent, if not of his claim for compensation, which made his contention impure? Was it not in the first place still the law of retribution which drove him to demand an explanation in proportion to his existence, a private explanation, a finite explanation?

As in literary tragedy, the final theophany has really explained nothing to him, but it has changed his view; he is ready to identify his freedom with inimical necessity; he is ready to convert freedom and necessity into fate. This conversion is the true "re-enactment"—no longer the material re-enactment which is still a kind of recompense and hence a sort of retribution, but the wholly internal re-enactment which is no longer restoration of an earlier happiness, but re-enactment of the present unhappiness. This is what is at stake after all: to renounce the law of retribution to the extent not only of ceasing to end the prosperity of the wicked, but of enduring misfortune as one accepts good fortune—that is to say, as God-given (Job 2:10). Such is the tragic wisdom of the re-enactment that triumphs over the ethical vision of the world.

What cannot be thought, what must not be uttered, can and must nevertheless be exhibited in the figure of the tragic hero; and that figure necessarily excited anew the great tragic emotions; for the nonposited aspect that any positing of evil involves can only awaken terror and compassion, beyond all judgment and all condemnation; a merciful vision of man comes to limit the accusation and save him from the wrath of the God who judges.

It is here that the tragic light cast upon biblical Judaism enhances the enigma of the serpent. In one sense, the figure of Satan throughout the Bible may be understood to represent the result of a process of development within the divine personality itself—whether Satan is viewed as a *malakh Yahweh* (Zech. 3:lff.) or even as an "independent" demon (I Chron. 21:1). It is even possible to see Satan ultimately as a factor in a divine process of differentiation, as a symbolic expression of man's inner spiritual reality, who arises and changes out of inner necessity, mirroring truths of the human spirit and its development. He may be seen to fill an intrinsic and dynamic role in the relationship between man and God—a role which has not lost its actuality even for modern Judaism.

But is it possible to absorb all the meanings revealed through that figure of Satan into the avowal of a purely human origin of evil? The figure of serpent, after all, is more than the transcendence of sin over sins, more than the nonposited, more than the radical of radical evil; the serpent is the Other, the Adversary, the pole of a counterparticipation, of a counterlikeness, about which one can say nothing except that the evil act, in positing itself, lets itself be seduced by the counterpositing of a source of iniquity represented by the Evil One, the Diabolical.

When tragedy shows the hero blinded by a demonic power, it manifests the demonic side of the human experience of evil by means of the tragic action; tragedy makes visible, without ever making thinkable, the situation of the wicked who can never occupy any but the second place in wickedness, "after" the Adversary.

Thus the tragic representation continues to express not only the reverse side of all confessions of sins, but the other pole of human evil; the evil for which I assume responsibility makes manifest a source of evil for which I cannot assume responsibility, but which I participate in every time that, through me, evil enters into the world as if for the first time. One might even argue that the avowal of evil as human calls forth a second-degree avowal, that of evil as nonhuman. Only tragedy can accept this avowal of the avowal and exhibit it in a spectacle as do so many imaginative texts of Scripture, for no coherent discourse can include that Other.

But perhaps there is more to be said: not only is something of tragic anthropology affirmed by the Bible, but something of tragic theology. The tragic element in biblical theology, for example, may even be discovered in the Psalms in the following way. If one narrows his sights and focuses initially on the ethical sense to which the Covenant between Israel and Yahweh was elevated, that ethical sense, which makes the Law the bond between man and God, may then be seen to react upon the conception of God himself; God becomes, and is, an ethical God. From the perspective of such a view, this "ethicization" of man and God tends, not surprisingly, toward a moral vision of the world, according to which history is a tribunal, pleasures and pains are retribution, God himself is a judge. At the same time, the whole of human experience assumes a penal character.

One may charge that this moral vision of the world, which the foregoing view asserts the Psalms present, was wrecked and demolished by Jewish thought itself when it meditated so exhaustively on the suffering of the innocent in the sapiential books of Scripture. May it even be possible that the innocent who suffer "needlessly" and with no comprehension of their condition bear witness to the irreducibility of the evil of scandal to the evil of fault, at least on the scale of human experience? How can a theory of retribution, which is a naïve expression of the moral vision of the world, account for all the unhappiness in the world? Is it not possible that the Hebrew themes of the "Suffering Just One" or the "Suffering Servant" lead back from the prophetic accusation to tragic pity?

Some of these very issues are raised still in almost all of the commentaries, critiques, and philosophical speculations of Jewish thinkers today. For Yehuda ha-Levi the very hierarchy of nature and the immediate and continuing act of God in creation made prophecy and prophetic accusation understandable; for Maimonides the influence of the Active intellect upon the imagination and the contemplation by reason of the imagery thus produced justified the prophet's claims and assertions. But today, one Jewish thinker after another seeks to turn back from "faith in the hidden God" and the "re-enactment" of misfortune to the prophetic tradition in order to see what tragedy contributes to the understanding of that tradition.

For many Jewish thinkers today, the prophetic tradition contributes two things: pity for human beings, who are nevertheless accused by the prophet; and fear and trembling before the divine abyss, before the God whose holiness is nevertheless proclaimed by the prophet.

Perhaps the possibility of the tragic God should never be

abolished altogether, so that biblical theology may be protected from the bare bones of ethical monotheism, with its Legislator and its Judge, continually confronting a moral subject who is endowed with complete and unfettered freedom. Perhaps the tragic theology of Judaism must always be possible, because suffering can no longer be understood only as a chastisement.

We must not grow weary of repeating that only he who confesses that he is the author of evil discovers the reverse of that confession; namely, the nonposited in the positing of evil, the Other temptation, and finally the incomprehensibility of God, who tests me and who can appear to me as my enemy. In this circular relation between Judaism and tragedy, Judaism is the right side and tragedy is the reverse side. But, above all, the polarity of the two betokens the arrest of human understanding at a certain stage.

At that stage our vision remains dichotomous; for although the evil that is committed leads to a just exile (that is what the figure of Adam represents), the evil that is suffered leads to an unjust deprivation; according to Rashi, Kara, Masnut, Sforno, and Maimonides, that is what the figure of Job represents. The first figure calls for the second; the second corrects the first.

Only a third figure could announce the transcending of the contradiction, and that would be the figure of the "Suffering Servant," who would make of suffering, of the evil that is undergone, an action capable of redeeming the evil that is committed. This enigmatic figure is the one celebrated by the Second Isaiah in the four "songs of the Servant of Yahwel" (Isaiah 42:1–9; 49:1–6; 50:4–11; 52:13–53: 12), and it opens up a perspective radically different from that of "wisdom." No longer is the issue one of the sufferer as symbol of sainthood, of rebellion against injustice, of confusion about Providence, of human imperfection, or as a scapegoat. Neither contemplation of creation nor its immense measure consoles; it is suffering itself. Suffering has become a gift that expiates the sins of the people.

Of course, there has been no lack of juridical exegetes in the history of Judaism who have understood substitutive suffering as a supreme way of salvaging the law of retribution. According to that scheme, the suffering which is a gift from God would be the means by which mercy would give "satisfaction" to justice. In this mechanical balancing of the divine attributes, justice and mercy, the new quality of the offered suffering is swallowed up again in the quantitative law of retribution.

In reality the suffering that is a gift takes up into itself the suffering that is a scandal, and thus inverts the relation of guilt to suffering. According to biblical law, guilt was supposed to produce suffering. Perhaps that is the reason finally that a stage of absurd suffering, the stage of Job, was needed, to mediate the movement from punishment to generosity, or as the Zoharic tradition expresses it, to become the spokesman for the redemptive quality of suffering.

That is why tragedy in Judaism has never finished dying. The theme of the wrath of God, the ultimate motive of the tragic consciousness, is invincible to the arguments of the philosopher as well as of the theologian. For there is no rational vindication of the innocence of God; every explanation of the Stoic or Leibnizian type is wrecked, like the naïve arguments of Job's friends, on the suffering of the innocent. They leave intact the opacity of evil and the opacity of the world; as soon as meaninglessness appears to swoop down intentionally on man, the schema of the wrath of God looms up and the tragic consciousness is once again restored.

2

Suffering and Redemption

In Judaism redemption is commonly understood as a special encounter with God in which we are aware at once of the awful holiness of God and of his inexhaustible gifts flowing from his Law. Essentially this encounter witnesses our relationship as persons covenanted with God and validates a renewal of life which proceeds from this reconciliation. But this reconciliation cannot be exhaustively described simply in terms of the relationship of the individual and God; for the renewal of life which proceeds therefrom finds expression in the recognition of a new relationship between man and man; the reconciliation with God is expressed in our lives in terms of a reconciliation with fellow man.

All this is rather homiletical and does not say anything that is not common knowledge in Judaism, whatever be the current differences in its practical interpretation. My remarks are purposely vague, so as to avoid involvement in controversies which would not be profitable at this stage. But one point emerges quite clearly: the characteristic features of our experience of redemption are essentially personal and subjective. At its core this experience involves personal covenant relationships of righteousness and love. If the meaning which we give to the term "redemption" is to be understood in the objective and efficacious light of our experience and enjoyment of it, redemption must retain its essentially personal character.

In this context questions of the kind that inquire as to

whether God should have created a universe in which there was no pain, or whether he should have removed all pain and suffering in the work of his continuing revelation, disguise the existential reality of the problem: they look like straightforward moral questions when, in fact, they are not. The idea of a painless Utopia strikes us as rather meaningful; it is appealing as a delightful source of entertainment to our imagination. But whether or not an imagined Paradise can be the subject of a serious moral judgment is another issue. This is a source of confusion which doubtless besets all discussions of the problem of suffering.

All suffering must, in one sense, be unequivocally condemned as evil—as a bad thing, as the opposite of blessedness. Otherwise it would not be suffering. But it does not follow that we can proceed from this to make moral judgments as to whether there ought or ought not to be such a thing as suffering in the universe of a just and good God. There is already in existence a vast body of literature which raises and attempts to resolve the bewildering question. I do not propose to enter into it. My point is, rather, that it is a fruitless discussion which arises out of a fundamentally meaningless question.

Since the question as to whether God should have removed all pain and suffering from the world is a moral question, it may be answered only by reference to one's own moral consciousness. But man's moral experience is such that some constitutive element of suffering always enters in, and not merely as an incidental factor, but, rather, as an element essential to the whole structure of our moral experience. Moral experience as we know it obliges that some element of resistance to the will be present—some desire left unsatisfied, some unpleasantness accepted—and it is this which gives reality to the moral struggle. Indeed, it is only from within the context of this negative obstacle of resistance to the will that the possibility of making moral judgments emerges at all. Therefore, even though we may be capable of imaginatively constructing a universe from which pain is absent, we cannot meaningfully make moral decisions about such a state of affairs.

What I am saying here must be distinguished from another kind of argument which says that since the possiblity of suffering is a function of, and necessarily prior to, the moral struggle, it is therefore morally acceptable that suffering should be present in the universe. My point is, rather, that since only in situations where suffering in one form or other is a factor to be reckoned with we can make moral decisions at all, any question as to whether suffering as such is morally good or bad is utterly bewildering and ultimately meaningless.

I may ask significantly why God should allow me to suffer in this particular way at this particular moment. But I cannot ask significantly why there should be suffering at all when I am discussing the life of moral persons. I can conceive of no serious moral decision without there being some element of cost to be reckoned with in the making of that decision.

Therefore, when we say, as it is our first impulse to do, that since God's covenants with us will involve a concern for our physical condition, the redemptive action of the Covenant relationship between God and man is to be expected to remove all human suffering and privation, we are making a judgment which at first sight seems obvious, but which comes to mean less and less the more we think about it.

The real problem is the vast amount of suffering which does not appear to belong to the moral structure of personal life at all. There is a vast difference, for instance, between the pains of martyrdom and the pains of a virulent and fatal disease. Both may lead to the final extremity of physical pain. But in the case of martyrdom, the pain fits significantly into a pattern of personal decision. The martyr can say: "I suffer this for the sake of . . ." The pain is no less painful, but it holds a significant place within the context of personal life and moral decision.

The extreme instance of pain manifesting itself as the hard core of resistance to the moral will makes the moral struggle real, while the pain of a disease is quite different. The pain of illness may be less painful, but it does not hold the same significant place within the context of moral decision. Such suffering may, of course, provide the occasion for the manifestation of magnificent qualities of personal courage, but this is only incidental; it does not in itself provide grounds for accepting the pain.

Some element of suffering, therefore, is essential to the structure of life as we know it. But if this is really so, why then do pain and frustration become a problem for the religious mind, and indeed for the mind of man generally? They become a problem precisely because they occasionally run counter to the redemptive goals of religious life when pain seems to negate human personality rather than to minister to it.

There are three main ways in which the frustrations of life take on this dysteleological or purposeless quality. First, there are natural calamities of all kinds, such as earthquakes and famines. Our impression of ruthless indifference is only reinforced by the picture of nature as a blind concatenation of mechanical cause-and-effect relationships. Second, there is the fact that man always seems doomed to frustration. Always man's reach seems to exceed his grasp; he solves one problem and another rises in its place; from the midst of one satisfaction another dissatisfaction is born; like Moses on Mount Nebo, he views the promised land and then inevitably hears the chilling words: "I have caused thee to see it with thine eyes, but thou shalt not go over thither." Third, there is the ubiquitous fact of death, which constitutes an apparent end of self.

Of these three ways in which suffering appears to frustrate the moral and redemptive goals of man, only the first is my primary concern at this early stage of my argument, since the immediate problem arises out of the relation of environment to self. The physical constitution of the world is an important factor in both the other aspects of suffering, but it does not enter into them in ways which could not be subsumed under a wide interpretation of the first point—namely, the impersonal nature of environment and its indifference to personal values.

In Scripture, God's providential care for the world he has made is expressed in such a way as to alter the problem of suffering for man in subtle ways. That care is depicted by the Psalmist with awe and gratitude:

> Who covereth the heaven with clouds, who prepareth rain for the earth, who maketh grass to grow upon the mountains. He giveth to the beast his food, and to the young ravens which cry.
>
> Psalm 147:8–9

The psalmists neither shut their eyes to the realities of suffering, nor do they ever imagine that man can be free of it. God satisfies all things in their season, but:

> Thou hidest thy face, they are troubled: thou takest away their breath, they die.
>
> Psalm 104:29

As the psalmists contemplate God's rule and care in nature, they never forget that nature is beyond man's control and that man is nothing in the sight of God. To this extent suffering and death present no problem; sickness or natural disasters never evoke questions which might lead to doubting the existence of God or to the working out of a theodicy. A denial of God's existence on intellectual grounds is outside the purview of biblical thought. The only kind of atheism it knows is a practical one:

> The fool hath said in his heart, there is no God. They are corrupt, they have done abominable works, there is none that doeth good.
>
> Psalm 14:1

The wicked ignore God by oppressing the widows and orphans and maltreating the lowly:

> The Lord shall not see, neither shall the God of Jacob regard it.
>
> Psalm 94:7

> How doth God know? and is there knowledge in the most High?
>
> Psalm 73:11

Belief in God's care is therefore poles apart from the Stoic doctrine of Providence, for which there is no precise counterpart in early biblical thought. Because Israel's theism is not based on a conviction of the harmonious unity of the cosmos, in which all separate things have their organic place and serve their purpose, we discover no attempt in it to ascertain the purpose and meaning behind misfortune and suffering; neither is there any suggestion that misfortune is illusory. The idea that everything is necessary when seen in the context of the whole, and is therefore good, is similary alien to Israelite thought. Israel knows that suffering is always suffering, and that every sufferer must bear his own burden. Torah never says, "Look at things as a whole," as did Marcus Aurelius; for doubt and anxiety are not be be banished by rational arguments of this sort. Man is not encouraged to think of himself simply as the particular instance of the universal. Instead, he is urged to look toward the future; if man cannot discover God in the present, he shall find God prospectively.

The problem, then, is not suffering in general, but the suffering of the righteous. If suffering can be explained as God's punishment for sin, why then do the righteous suffer? And why do so many of the wicked prosper? The common biblical answer to these questions is that the wicked will suffer and the righteous prosper at the completion of time.

> Fret not thyself because of evil men, neither be thou envious at the wicked; for there shall be no reward to the evil man; the candle of the wicked shall be put out.
>
> Proverbs 24:19–20

> For evil doers shall be cut off: But those that wait upon the Lord, they shall inherit the earth. For yet a little while, and the wicked shall not be; yea, thou shalt diligently consider his place, and it shall not be.
>
> Psalm 37:9–10

This answer does not satisfy all Israelites, for it is all too often refuted by experience. Consequently we occasionally hear biblical expressions of resignation: life is like that; some prosper, others suffer misfortune:

> The poor and the deceitful man meet together: the Lord lighteneth both their eyes.
>
> Proverbs 29:13

This mood of resignation finds classical expression in Ecclesiastes:

> Vanity of vanities, saith the Preacher, vanity of vanities; all is vanity. What profit hath a man of all his labour which he taketh under the sun? One generation passeth away, and another generation cometh: but the earth abideth for ever. . . . The thing that hath been, it is that which shall be; and that which is done is that which shall be done: and there is no new thing under the sun.
>
> Ecclesiastes 1:2–4, 9

> . . . the work that is wrought under the sun is grievous unto me: for all is vanity and vexation of spirit.
>
> Ecclesiastes 2:17

> There is nothing better for a man, than that he should eat and drink, and that he should make his soul enjoy good in his labour. . . . eat thy bread with joy, and drink thy wine with a merry heart; . . . Let thy garments always be white; and let thy head lack no ointment. Live joyfully with the wife whom thou lovest all the days of the life of thy vanity, which he hath given thee under the sun.
>
> Ecclesiastes 2:24; 9:7–9

If such resignation comes uncomfortably close to practical atheism, one experiences the opposite extreme in the book of Job. Job wrestles with the problem of suffering, and comes tortuously to the conclusion that the only possible response left open obliges him to submit uncomplainingly to the will of God. God's wisdom surpasses all human understanding. When his friends insist that Job's suffering must be the punishment of some sin he has committed, he protests innocence; and as he contemplates, he realizes that God is oppressing him like a tyrant.

> Whom, though I were righteous, yet would I not answer, but I would make my supplication to my judge. If I had called, and he had answered me; yet would I not believe that he had hearkened unto my voice. For he breaketh me with a tempest, and multiplieth my wounds without cause. He will not suffer me to take my breath, but filleth me with bitterness. If I speak of strength, lo, he is strong: and if of judgment, who shall set me a time to plead? If I justify myself, mine own mouth shall condemn me: if I say, I am perfect, it shall also prove me perverse.
>
> Job 9:15–20

Even that does not quiet his heart. He must insist on justice from God, seeking neither retribution nor reward, but recognition.

> Surely, I would speak to the Almighty, and I desire to reason with God.
>
> Job 13:3

God refuses such advocates, so anxious to prove himself in the right by proving Job in the wrong!

> Will ye speak wickedly for God, and talk deceitfully for him? Will ye accept his person? will ye contend for God?
>
> Job 13:7–8

> Oh that I knew where to find him! that I might come even to his seat! I would order my cause before him, and fill my mouth with arguments.
>
> Job 23:3–4

He begs God to let him have his accusation in black and white, to clarify its terms so that he can refute it.

> Surely I would take it upon my shoulder, and bind it as a crown to me. I would declare unto him the number of my steps; as a prince would I go near unto him.
>
> Job 31:36–37

God accepts the challenge, appears to Job from the whirlwind, and gives him his answer, which takes the form of a counterquestion:

> Where wast thou when I laid the foundations of the earth? declare, if thou hast understanding. Who hath laid the measures thereof, if thou knowest? or who hath stretched the line upon it? . . . Wilt thou also disannul my judgment? wilt thou condemn me, that thou mayest be righteous? Hast thou an arm like God? or canst thou thunder with a voice like him? Deck thyself now with majesty and excellence; and array thyself with glory and beauty. . . . Then will I also confess unto thee that thine own right hand can save thee.
>
> Job 38:4–5; 40:8–10, 14

Job is reduced to silence:

> Behold, I am vile; what shall I answer thee? I will lay my hand upon my mouth. Once have I spoken; but I will not answer: yea, twice, but I will proceed no further.
>
> Job 40:4–5

Confronted by God's omnipotence and unfathomable wisdom, man's only recourse is to hold his peace. The problem of suffering per se has no solution, for inductive reason is entirely cut off when man is obliged to make his submission to God. The author of Job illustrates this point by placing his poem in the framework of the traditional story of Job as a religious man who, when all was taken from him, says meekly: "Naked came I out of my mother's womb, and naked shall I return thither: the Lord gave, and the Lord hath taken away; blessed by the name of the Lord" (1:21). And when his wife pours scorn on him: "What? shall we receive good at the hand of the Lord, and shall we not receive evil?" (2:10).

To be sure, the book of Job is an exception in the Bible, for here the conventional picture of God's righteousness as witnessed in the fortunes of men breaks down. The author has discovered that even the righteous must suffer. Yet he keeps within the limits of biblical thought; he does not doubt God; and although his conception of God provides no clue to the problem of suffering, he does not abandon it on that account. Indeed, his account accentuates it when he asserts that the omnipotence of God is infinite, and the wisdom in his apparent caprice surpasses all comprehension; all man can do is hold his peace.

This is perhaps the most extreme statement of a proposition of faith found everywhere in the Bible: submission to God's unfathomable purpose. Such acquiescence is often found linked with a confidence that God will redress the situation in the future, particularly if man is content to renounce his self-will and wait quietly upon God. Thus there grows up a unique conception of faith: to believe in God is not simply to believe in his existence, but meekly to submit to his will and wait upon him in quietness and confidence. That is what the Psalmist means when he says:

> Nevertheless I am continually with thee: thou hast holden me by my right hand. Thou shalt guide me with thy counsel, and afterward receive me to glory. Whom have I in heaven but thee? and there is none upon earth that I desire beside thee. My flesh and my heart faileth: but God is the strength of my heart, and my portion for ever. For lo, they that are far from thee shall perish; thou hast destroyed all that go a-whoring from thee. But it is good for me to draw near to God: I have put my trust in the Lord God, . . .
>
> Psalm 73:23–8

And when Jeremiah complains:

> Woe is me, my mother, that thou hast borne me a man of strife and a man of contention to the whole earth! I have neither lent on usury,

> nor men have lent to me on usury; yet every one of them doth curse me.

God answers:

> Verily it shall be well with thy remnant; verily I will cause the enemy to entreat thee well in the time of evil and in the time of affliction. Shall iron break the northern iron and the steel?
>
> Jeremiah 15:10–12

The religious man can still fly to God in prayer and find refuge and consolation. "He lifts up his eyes unto the hills from whence cometh help" (cf. Pss. 121; 25:1–2; 62:5–7).

But biblical response to the problem of suffering elsewhere exhibits subtle alterations related to Israel's corporate status. Because pious Israelites know that their destiny as individuals is bound up with that of the nation, part of the sufferings which fall to the lot of individuals are inextricably bound up with the sufferings of the nation; moreover, discussions concerning the fate of the nation throw the question of God's righteousness into bold relief. Sometimes this feature fades into the background, as in the case of Ecclesiastes, Job, and many of the psalms. Elsewhere, however, it receives great prominence. One response is that found in the denunciations of the prophets. Israel's sufferings are usually interpreted in terms of divine punishment and God's intention to correct a recalcitrant people; the nation's sufferings must therefore be willingly borne. The nation must "turn" so that God can turn to it again. But besides these prophetic admonitions and threats, there are also passages which promise a good time coming, when God will create his people anew.

The sufferings of the nation must be faced in a way similar to those faced by individuals—by meekly submitting to the will of God, by waiting and trusting in him.

> For thus saith the Lord, the holy One of Israel; In returning and rest shall ye be saved; in quietness and in confidence shall be your strength: and ye would not. But ye said, No; for we will flee upon horses: therefore shall they that pursue you be swift.
>
> Isaiah 30:15–16

> If ye will not believe, surely ye shall not be established.
>
> Isaiah 7:9

He that believeth shall not make haste.

Isaiah 28:16

In both cases—individual and corporate—ideas of order and purpose are absent from the universe. In their place, we discover promises of a future kingdom to be established by God. That is the biblical answer to the problem of theodicy, insofar as there is any answer at all. God confronts man with his blessings and demands, judging him in each successive moment. Every such moment, however, points toward the future; for God is always a "participial" God who is expected to come, ever transcending the here and now. But this transcedence (there is no actual word for it in the Bible) is neither a metaphysical transcendence of spirit over matter nor a transcendence of the world of ideas over the world of growth and decay. For the religion of ancient Israel, everything turns on how seriously a man is prepared to take this idea of a God who is always "in the process" of coming and how he interprets it. Is he prepared to await an eschatological Day of the Lord in every future moment? Or does he expect the future to result in a historically felicitous ending, inaugurating for himself and the nation a state of permanent bliss in this world? If the exegetical choice were made in favor of fulfillment within history, would that not reduce God's transcendence to a meaningless secularization within this world? That would doubtless mean the end of faith. The only way out of this dilemma would be to introduce a life after death to rescue faith. But such a notion was foreign to ancient Israel; it emerged gradually, even reluctantly, in postexilic Judaism, leaving its sole traces in a few quite late passages in the Bible and the Apocrypha.

One may now more easily see how certain aspects of the problem of suffering may be categorically subsumed under the more general problem of the relationship between the personal and the impersonal. Man's longing and prayers have not been directed at domesticating a world with all the harmless properties of a padded cell. The sufferings from which man has sought redemption have always been those arising from impersonal events and qualities in the world which obtruded upon and frustrated his life as a personal being—the great mass movement of expanding empires which had ceased to be the expression of a personal society and had become an impersonal force, taking no account of the moral dedication of the small nation of Israel to a holy God; the unaccountable caprices of the elements of nature; the visitation of disease; the fateful and inexorable movements of the heavenly bodies as witnessing the impersonal determinism of the forces to which man's life was subject; the mechanical determinism of the universe of Isaac Newton. Immanuel Kant's more recent formulation of the problem in the antinomy of practical reason refers us in more general terms to the same aspect of our environment–the impersonal structure of the world and the indifference of its laws to personal moral values. Even Hegel's framing of the same problem in terms of "unhappy consciousness" alludes in a subtler way to the same factors in our experience.

So long as we think of the impersonal forces which obtrude upon man's personal life only as external factors that frustrate the realization of his purposes in the world, we have not felt the full weight of this problem. The kind of solution which one discovers in the early Gnostics and in Kant tries to restrict the problem within these limits. Their solution may be pessimistic in that it despairs entirely of this universe as a suitable place for the full realization of man's life as person; yet at the same time it does offer hope of salvation of a kind.

The sharp distinction between "the starry heavens without" and "the moral law within" may be the source of Kant's despair as it is expressed in the antinomy of practical reason; but at the same time the very sharpness of the distinction endows the inward life of self with a kind of isolated, unassailable security. If only one can be assured that the moral law and the center of personal life which it implies are unassailably locked up "within," and the menacingly impersonal structure of the world and the heavenly bodies are entirely "without," so that though it may in some degree frustrate the purposes of self it can never seriously menace the essentially inward life of self, there is real comfort in this assurance. This is the religious source of appeal of Kant's formulation, and of the widespread acceptance of this kind of world-view in some forms of pietistic Judaism.

But this happy assurance of the inward security of self,

whatever may be the frustrations that come from without, must always be qualified by the knowledge that it is in this world and in some sense as part of it that we exist. This forces upon us the realization that the impersonal structure of the world not merely frustrates the personal life of self from without, but even negates the inner integrity of free, personal selfhood. At its simplest level this realization consists of the recognition that physically man is only a minute particle in this vast, impersonal system. The inward threat which this fact offers to the life of self is expressed in the fear which it engenders that perhaps our life of personal decision is somehow only an illusion.

At the level of philosophic inquiry there are many cogent arguments with which to allay such a fear. But the moment of despair in which this fear is an actual, lived experience remains real and frightening and is by no means confined to the philosophers, though others may not be so articulate in their verbal expression of if. One may, for instance, in a moment of bereavement look upon the "last remains"—all that has been left by the relentless progress of natural forces as they cut right across a personal life, so obviously a dead thing and not a person anymore—and experience the despairing fear that perhaps all the inwardness of personal life is merely a brief illusion which finally fades again into the impersonal structure of the universe. Or again, the awe which Immanuel Kant admitted he experienced when he contemplated the "starry heavens without" was not merely the outcome of his philosophic inquiry. Despite the extreme austerity of his emotional life, he there expressed something of that sense of personal insecurity which we all sometimes feel in the face of so terrifying a vista.

This brings us to a point where we can see more clearly the revelance of modern Jewish analyses of the difficulties of giving an account of the place of the self in existence, which arose out of what may at the time have appeared as a tedious and unnecessary criticism of Hegel. If only one could give an account of the relation of self and world in terms of simple disjunction or conjunction, the menace which the impersonal structure of the world offers to the personal life of all Jews would not be so serious. If the relation of self and world could be described in the same way as we describe objects, then the inner nature of self could be regarded as unaffected by the impersonal nature of the world.

Self and world could be regarded as two distinct natures coexisting and only externally related to one another in a contingency relationship. The outward realization of the purposes of self might be frustrated by the impersonal nature of the world, but its inner nature would remain secure. But when it is realized that the relation of self and world cannot ultimately be thus described and that self and world are correlative terms, two consequences follow. For me the source of the Kantian type of dualism is removed so that at least the possibility of integrating man's experience of the natural world with his inner moral life remains open. For another it may open up the possibility that man's inner life as person, as well as his outward expression of that life in purposeful activity, may be overwhelmed by the impersonal structure of the world.

The ground of personal anxiety about the place of the self vis-à-vis existence, as I have tried to describe it, turns out to be just this conflict between the personal and the impersonal in the correlation of self and world. It is the totality of "given" experience which constitutes my awareness of the world as over against me; yet it is also that same totality which I recognize as constituting my concrete existence as self. All experience is both inward and outward at the same time. Ultimately the outward structure of experience as my world is correlative with its inward structure as myself.

Therefore the inward structure of self does not remain unaffected by the impersonal structure of its world. This is the problem of the "redemption of self into self and not-self" which became so hopelessly confused in the nineteenth century with a purely logical problem about the relations of universal and particular in Hegel's treatment of it. In reality it is simply this problem of the conflict of the personal and the impersonal in the correlation of self and world. This at least shows that the tension between the personal and the impersonal functions as a constant, appearing in the particular formulations of the problem with which I have been dealing and have raised thus far.

3

Election and Calamity

Biblical religion was a national religion. The life of the community and its religion formed a unity; God and the nation belonged together and were the outcome of a particular history: Moses in the wilderness had welded a number of nomadic tribes into a nation whose bond of unity was the worship of Yahweh: Israel's wars were Yahweh's wars, Israel's glory his glory. The land which Israel conquered belonged to Yahweh, though he gave it to the nation for their heritage.

In time of peace he was the Lord of the whole life of the community and its patron of justice. By his name men used to swear, and in his name they made treaties. This relationship with God was conceived in terms of a Covenant, where God was the major party. But by offering it to the people, God entered into mutual obligations with them. He dealt with the people as a corporate entity, not with its individual members—or more precisely, he dealt with the male members of the community.

The nation bound itself to worship only Yahweh, and Yahweh bound himself to succour and protect the nation. This Covenant was inaugurated by a sacrifice and was perpetuated through the cultus. It was irrevocable so long as the cultus was duly performed. Quite soon, however, the prophets raised their protest against the popular conception of the Covenant.

As a consequence of the occupation of Canaan and the influence of Canaanite religion, there was a very real danger of Israel coming to believe that God was tied to the land. If unchecked, this Canaanite influence would have destroyed the distinctive feature of the Hebrew religion and would have made it just like any of the other Semitic faiths. In these religions the deity was tied to the land, with its mountains and fields, its vegetation. Their gods were worshiped as powers of fertility, as divine forces at work in nature. It was just this idea that the prophets set out to combat. According to them, God was not tied to the land, but to the nation, an idea sharing certain affinities with the Greek religion of the city-state. But Israel never regarded herself as a *polis* or city-state in the Greek sense. The city-state was constituted by the total will of a community of free citizens, a will providing the norm of community life. Its deity was conceived as the guardian of this norm, and hence as the personification of the will of the community; therefore the problem which constantly beset the city-state: Would this idea of community continue to maintain its priority over the individual? Or would the community come to be thought of as derivative from the individual, as the product of the subjective will of its individual members? Even today this remains a key problem of democracy.

Such a problem, however, never arose in Israel, because there the nation was never conceived as the result of the individual will of its members, developing its own life as the city-state; rather, the nation was the product of a will operating in history: the problem was one of loyalty to history. Since the contemporary scene was always the product of a past it had not itself created, history was not the story of man's exploits and achievements, but a gift—the sign of God's grace. "And say thou not in thy heart, 'My power and the might of my hand hath gotten me this wealth.' But thou shalt remember the Lord thy God: for it is he that giveth thee power to get wealth . . ." (Deut. 8:17–18).

The emergence of the nation might therefore be described as an act of creation. Moreover, the deliverance from Egypt was depicted as the destruction of the dragon in primeval times (Isa. 51:9–10). Similarly, national calamity was depicted as the return of chaos.

According to the Bible, the nation is not constituted by the forces and purposes inherent in it at any given time, but through the mighty acts of God in the past. It was he who brought the nation out of Egypt and made his Covenant with it on Mount Sinai. It was he who led it through the wilderness and gave it the land—the land which is now its heritage, the land of its fathers. These fathers are not dim figures of a distant past, but the abiding witnesses of the nation's history.

This sense of history was reflected in the principal feasts. Originally the festivals of a pastoral and agricultural people, they were transformed into historical commemorations. The Passover was originally the New Year feast, when the firstborn of the herd was presented to the deity. In ancient Palestine this was combined with the *matzoth,* the feast of the first-fruits, when the sickle was put to the corn. Later, however, it was transformed into the commemoration of the Exodus, when the Hebrew tribes became a nation and national history began. The Feast of Weeks began as the thanksgiving for the corn harvest. Later it became the commemoration of the giving of the Law on Mount Sinai. The Feast of the Tabernacles, originally another New Year's festival and the Feast of the Ingathering (the thanksgiving at the end of the harvest as a whole), was later transformed into the commemoration of the time when Israel dwelt in tents in the wilderness.

Unlike the cult legends of classical Greece and the Hellenistic period, the legends associated with the feasts do not tell of the fate of the deity, but of the history of the nation. The cult itself lost much of its former magical associations as a means of securing the prosperity of the nation and its land. There are indeed traces of such notions in the rites of purification and atonement. But the important thing about the feasts is that they became themselves moments in the redemptive history. In the feasts, that fulfilled history becomes a present reality in which all the participants share.

This belief in the historical origins of the Covenant finds its theological expression in the doctrine of election—the election of Israel. Here the underlying idea is that the nation owes all it has and is, not to itself, but to God who rules its history. Moreover, Israel's election does not rest on its own merits:

> Speak not thou in thy heart, after the Lord thy God hath cast out the nations before thee, saying, "For my righteousness the Lord hath

> brought me in to possess this land". . . . Not for thy righteousness, or for the uprightness of thine heart, dost thou go to possess this land. . . .
>
> Deuteronomy 9:4–5

The divine election is unmotivated, gratuitous, and free, so that Israel is perpetually dependent upon the grace of God, while its election is beyond its control. God's mighty acts in the past never become an assured possession; they must be appropriated ever anew. To observe the terms of its Covenant, Israel is obliged to be loyal to its history. This sense of calling and election is, in its original form, a conscious determination to remain loyal to history, with all the blessings and responsibilities that such an obligation entails.

Israel can rely on the faithfulness of God, but only on condition that it remains faithful itself. Its faithfulness is demonstrated first and foremost in the cultus. It is here that Israel acknowledges its God and its history:

> A Syrian ready to perish was my father, and he went down into Egypt, and sojourned there with a few, and became there a nation, great, mighty and populous: And the Egyptians evil entreated us and afflicted us, and laid us upon hard bondage: And when we cried unto the Lord God of our Fathers, the Lord heard our voice, and looked on our affliction, and our labour, and our oppression: And the Lord brought us forth out of Egypt with mighty hand, and with an outstretched arm, and with great terribleness, and with signs, and with wonders: And he hath brought us into this land, even a land flowing with milk and honey. And now, behold, I have brought the first fruits of the land, which thou, O Lord, hast given me.
>
> Deuteronomy 26:5–10

It is loyalty to history that the prophets exhort:

> Yet destroyed I the Amorite before them, . . . Also I brought you up from the land of Egypt, and led you forty years through the wilderness, to possess the land of the Amorite. And I raised up of your sons for prophets, and of your young men for Nazarites. Is it not even thus, O ye children of Israel? saith the Lord.
>
> Amos 2:9–11

Israel's disloyalty is denounced as adultery by the prophets: the Covenant is compared to a marriage, the election of Israel to an espousal (Hosea, Jeremiah).

Loyalty consists in the due performance of the cultus and in offering it exclusively to Yahweh. But loyalty also—and with the prophets particularly if not exclusively so—consists in obedience to the Law of Yahweh, which embraces the whole life of the nation, requiring above all righteousness and justice. With their exhortations to constancy and uprightness, the prophets combat the security of national pride. If God chose Israel, he can also reject her:

> Woe to them that are at ease in Zion, and trust in the mountain of Samaria. Gather yourselves, ye firstlings of the nations, . . . Pass ye to Calneh, and see; and from thence go to Hamath the great: then go down to Gath of the Philistines: be they better than these kingdoms? or their border greater than your border?
>
> Amos 6:1–2

> Hear this word that the Lord hath spoken against you, O children of Israel, against the whole family which I brought up from the land of Egypt, saying, You only have I known of all the families of the earth; therefore I will punish you for all your iniquities!
>
> Amos 3:1–2

> Are ye not as children of the Ethiopians unto me, O children of Israel? saith the Lord. Have I not brought up Israel out of the land of Egypt? and the philistines from Caphtor, and the Syrians from Kir?
>
> Amos 9:7

> Yet I am the Lord thy God from the land of Egypt, and thou shalt know no God but me: for there is no savior beside me. I did know thee in the wilderness, in the land of great drought. When they came to the pasture, they were filled; they were filled, and their heart was exalted; therefore they have forgotten me. Therefore I will be unto them as a lion: as a leopard by the way will I observe them.
>
> Hosea 13:4–7

God will exact terrible vegeance on disloyalty. He will destroy his faithless people. Perhaps a remnant will be left and will "turn"; but judgment will come upon the nation as a whole, and will be wrought out in history. It is God who has called Assyria as the chastening rod to smite Ephraim and Judah. It is God who raises the king of Babylon to destroy Jerusalem. As for King Manasseh's idolatry (698–643 B.C.E.):

> Therefore thus saith the Lord God of Israel, Behold I am bringing such evil upon Jerusalem and Judah, that whosoever heareth of it, both his ears shall tingle. And I will stretch over Jerusalem the line of Samaria, and the plummet of the house of Ahab: and I will wipe Jerusalem as a

> man wipeth a dish, wiping it, and turning it upside down. And I will forsake the remnant of mine inheritance, and deliver them into the hand of their enemies; Because they have done that which was evil in my sight, and have provoked me to anger, since the day that their fathers came forth out of Egypt, even unto this day.
>
> II Kings 21:12–15

According to the traditional view, God exercises his power on behalf of Israel; but in the prophets' view, he can also exercise his power *against* Israel, and owing to the people's wickedness will actually do so. Logically this means the end of national religion. The more the prophets emphasize ethical obedience as opposed to the performance of the cultus as the *sine qua non* for the maintenance of the Covenant, the more they abandon the old sense of the latter. If the Covenant depends primarily on loyalty to history, its maintenance is bound to be always in doubt.

Thus, in the last resort, the past poses a disconcerting problem to the nation: the Covenant can never be fully realized until the future. It can never have been concluded definitively in the past, nor can its permanence be secured by the performance of the cultus. If, as the naïve view supposed, the security of the individual rests on his membership in the elect nation, then conversely, according to the prophetic view, the gratuitous election of the people depends on the individual's obedience to the demands of God.

And the less that is the case in the empirical course of history, the more the Covenant develops into an eschatological concept. In other words, the Covenant is not capable of realization in actual history; its authentic realization becomes conceivable only in some mythical future of redemption.

> Behold, the days come, saith the Lord, that I will make a new covenant with the house of Israel, and with the house of Judah: Not according to the covenant I made with their fathers in the day that I took them by the hand to bring them out of the land of Egypt; which my covenant they brake, and I rejected them. But this is the covenant that I will make with the house of Israel; After those days, saith the Lord, I will put my law in their inward parts, and write it in their hearts; and will be their God, and they shall be my people. And they shall teach no more every man his neighbor, and every man his brother, saying, Know the Lord: for they shall all know me, from the

> least of them unto the greatest of them, saith the Lord: for I will forgive their iniquity, and I will remember their sin no more.
>
> Jeremiah 31:31–34

> Moreover I will make a covenant of peace with them; it shall be an everlasting covenant with them: and I will multiply them, and will set my sanctuary in the midst of them for everymore. My tabernacle shall also be with them: yea, I will be their God, and they shall be my people. And the heathen shall know that I the Lord do sanctify Israel, when my sanctuary shall be in the midst of them for evermore.
>
> Ezekiel 37:26–28

The actual course of Israel's history, the settlement of nomadic pastoral tribes in Canaan, made Israel a nation of agriculturists. This brought the nation into contact with foreign cultures. It was these influences which turned them eventually into a national state, thus involving them in political relations with other nations, both great and small, in the semicircle between Egypt and Babylon. All this meant danger to the religion of Yahweh. With the tilling of the soil, customs from the fertility cults of foreign nations, and even those cults themselves, found their way into Israel. Political change brought social upheaval in its train, with a consequent lowering of moral standards. Social differences began to emerge, and social sins to abound.

In protesting against this moral decline, the prophets also raised their voice against the foreign cults and the customs which came in from them. Unfortunately, however, the prophets combined their preaching of social righteousness with a protest against all forms of secular and materialistic progress. They called for a return to a golden age of the past, to the simple life before the state began. They depicted that age as a time when the holy people were faithful to the Covenant and lived at peace with God—a Utopian requirement in view of the actual course of history; Israel was so small that she was unable to pursue an independent policy of her own, especially after the schism between the northern and southern kingdoms. And then came the exile, as a result of which the Utopian policy of the prophets gained the upper hand, and an attempt was made to put the idea of a holy people into practice.

Like other Semitic nations, Israel regarded God as her king.

His will was law for his people. He was the judge and arbiter in all disputes, the patron of justice at home and the wager of Israel's wars abroad. At the New Year's feast, his accession to the throne was celebrated with the cry: "Yahweh is king!" The hymns sung at the feast praised him as the God exalted above all other gods and as Lord of the world. His kingship became a present reality through the performance of the cultus.

With Israel having thus become a state and with the institution of monarchy, a conflict arose between the kingship of Yahweh and that of the earthly monarch. The prophets resisted the introduction of monarchy. The story in I Samuel 8:lff. records how the elders came to Saul at Ramah and demanded: "Make us a king to judge us like other nations. . . . But the thing displeased Samuel." And when he prayed to the Lord, the Lord answered him: "Hearken unto the voice of the people in all that they say unto thee: for they have not rejected thee, but they have rejected me, that I should reign over them." The prophets dated all Israel's sin from the day that Saul was crowned king at Gilgal: "All their wickedness was done in Gilgal: for there I hated them" (Hos. 9:15).

With the prosperity during David's reign, the monarchy became so popular that his reign was later regarded as a golden age. When the time of salvation came, there would be a new Davidic king. But at the outset, the earthly monarchy was regarded as a threat to the kingship of God. The old tribal structure was replaced by a new provincial organization, which met the technical requirements of an organized state. A new aristocracy of bureaucrats and officers came into being, and the army, which hitherto had been a popular muster, now consisted of professional soldiers. This made it necessary to raise taxes, as we hear in I Samuel 8:10–18. In addition, the kings of Israel were obliged to seek treaties with other nations.

Yahweh became the God of the state and a temple was built for him in accordance with Canaanite custom. National shrines were erected at Jerusalem, Bethel, and Samaria. With the redistribution of wealth, the old communal law of village life declined, and the administration of justice became uncertain. Among the ruling classes, the old inhibitions disappeared with the old moral sanctions and there were ceaseless complaints about injustice and violence.

The prophets fulminated against the new institutions and their moral consequences, but they failed to perceive the necessities of state. If kings were willing to accept the responsibilities of government, they were simply not in a position to follow the ideals of the prophets. They were bound to be anxious about defense. They had to ensure that the state was strong, and to that end they had to enter into foreign alliances. For their part, the prophets were equally incapable of presenting their ideals in such a way as to make them practical politicians in the new situation. Their demand of righteousness and justice would in itself have been practicable in any proper kind of state, but when associated with a demand for a return to the old family, clan, and tribal organization, they were doomed to failure at the outset. And when they sought to uphold the sovereignty of God by denying the right of the state to administer justice, and insisting that the judicial functions should be placed in the hands of the priestly caste, they were undermining the very foundation of the state.

When Israel lost her independence at the exile, the Utopia of the prophets lived on and became the mainstay of the nation in its bondage to foreign rule. To begin with, the old aristocratic order of the patriarchs was re-established, though this was increasingly supplanted by the rule of the priestly caste. Israel was now organized on a hierarchical basis, with the high priest as its head.

In this way, the theocratic ideal of the sovereign rule of God was realized at last—but at a cost. Israel ceased to be a nation and became a church. All the functions of government, except the administration of justice, which remained in the hands of the priests, were managed by the foreign power. Cyrus, who restored the Jews from exile, was hailed by the devout as the Lord's anointed. Ezra (444 B.C.E.), under a direct commission from the Persian emperor, set up the Jewish church-state, which was peculiar in that Israel was at once a church and a national community.

As a national community, Jewish society derived its cohesion from the tradition of its past, preserving its national distinctiveness through its ritual. Hence the importance of circumcision and the Sabbath. Israel looked for a return of the old days when she had been an independent state, for a restoration of the kingdom of David. But that could not be brought about by direct political actions. It had to be left to supernatural intervention. In fact, the new kingdom of David was not to be a real state on earth at all.

Thus the conception of a holy nation with God as its king was realized in the peculiar form of a church-state. Any other possibility was out of the question if the people of God were to be identified with any empirical community. This is shown by the way in which the full realization of the ideal of the holy people, together with that of the Covenant, was projected into a historical future. The genuine idea of God as a God who was to come was abandoned, and with it the conception of God as the Lord of history. In the eschatological hope, history was expected to come to an end. By its anticipation of the eschatological future, Israel lost its historical moorings. This it did by molding the ritual pattern of its whole life in such a way as to emphasize its distinctiveness from all other nations as the holy people of God.

The moral element in the conception of Yahweh, which had been present from the beginning, found its clearest expression in the religion of the prophets from the sixth to the eighth centuries B.C.E.

One of the most significant features of this prophetic movement is illustrated in the opening chapter of Amos, where nationality is transcended and moral standards are applied to man as man, of whatever nation. Hosea brings out the deeper thought of the importance of the inner attitudes as the source of conduct. Out of his personal experience of sorrowful love, he enters into the very heart of God's grace. Micah shares the more democratic outlook of the desert in his attitude toward the oppressed poor. In relation to man, as in the relation to God, the essentials of life are moral. Another aspect of the morality of the prophets from Hosea onward is seen in their attitude toward idols. This, I think, can be regarded as the negative side of their positive emphasis on morality. Implicitly, at least, the prophets substituted their own moral consciousness for the material image as the means of approach to God, and of the realization of his presence. The "ethical theism" of the prophets found its necessary sanctions through the interpretation of current events and of the background of political history.

A widespread and general confidence in the divine election of Israel was manifest; this was as true for the prophet who moralized it as for the people who materialized it, notwithstanding the repeated disappointment of political hopes, after the transient successes under David and Solomon, and finally, the two captivities and the cessation of political independence. The faith of the prophets, in both quality and quantity, is seen in their refusal to accept such events as implying any failure of the divine purpose. They persistently reinterpreted that purpose to meet the new denials of it. They regarded political overthrow or social disaster as the penalty for social immorality, so that what had seemed to hide God really revealed him.

In wisdom literature (the sapiential books of the Bible), prophetic morality is transferred from national to individual application, together with the doctrine of divine retribution. "Wisdom" also supplies us with the nearest approach to a systemization of Hebrew ethics, which is characterized by the very close interrelation of morality and religion, the conception of morality as revealed law, the emphasis on the will of the individual and on the social righteousness of the community (this last is apparently a development of the corporate personality of the nomadic clan, clarified in the moral consciousness of the prophets).

Just as wisdom writers are responsible for the individualized application of prophetic morality, so from them comes the challenge to the doctrine of divine retribution. So long as men were treated in the mass, whether as nations or as families, it was possible to assert with plausibility that complete divine retribution would come, sooner or later, within this unit. But after Jeremiah and Ezekiel had placed a new emphasis on the individual, which the wise men had continued and developed, it became apparent to some thinkers at least that the doctrine of retribution broke down when applied simply within the span of the individual life.

The authors of Proverbs and Ecclesiastes challenge the doctrine of retribution; the former with belief in some hidden divine purpose which would explain and justify the experience of life; the latter as a pessimist and agnostic, though not an atheist. Finally the wisdom literature makes a very important contribution to the conception of "mediation" between God and man. Personified Wisdom is conceived as the companion and helper of God in the creation of the world, which exhibits his wisdom while she continues to inspire men with the qualities that make for right and successful life, in the individual and the society.

"The Day of the Lord shall be darkness, and not light" (Amos 5:18).

The Day of the Lord is here an eschatological concept, derived, apparently, from the association of two ideas–that of a day of victory in battle (when a god's power was demonstrated) and that of a high day of cult festival (when a god's power was celebrated). Both were critical occasions in the people's common experience. The popular expectation which Amos rejected was evidently that of an approaching day when Israel's enemies would be overthrown, and her peace and prosperity assured. This victory would manifest God's power over the forces of primeval chaos which preceded his beneficent creation. This latter was an important element in Israel's mythology, annually celebrated, in all probability, on the day of the New Year festival.

The prophets certainly declared its imminence, as they revised its meaning. They felt that God must show himself soon because the moral and religious situation demanded it, and unheeded afflictions gave warning of the approach of final catastrophe. God was about to show himself in his unmistakable character, by action. Israel would be brought face to face with the awful reality of his righteousness, and then her sinful condition, not her past privileges, would determine the outcome. At the very least, she would be chastised. But the coming of God meant the presence of his mercy as well as of his righteousness; it would sift out the good as surely as it would the evil. It would be a day of salvation (said Isaiah and Hosea), as well as of trouble, of mercy quick to overtake judgment.

But in Amos and Zephaniah there is little hint of mercy, perhaps because the starkest kind of contrast to the popular expectation was felt to be necessary. But even in Amos there is the suggestion that total destruction might yet be averted through complete redirection of the community's life; though this is a logical concession, apparently, rather than a hope. Zephaniah, too, admits the possibility—but only as a possibility—that faithful individuals may escape. In Isaiah this becomes the well-known doctrine of the remnant, the spiritual kernel of the nation which has "survival value" in the eyes of the Lord. The remnant's determining characteristic is its faithfulness, and the patient waiting which shows unshaken trust. On these conditions only, may men join the company of those whom disaster cannot overwhelm. In Hosea and Jeremiah the thought of God's mercy is most impressive; but Hosea speaks, too, of God's withdrawal until Israel repents, and Jeremiah of inevitable chastisement. God's healing mercy will be present even in his judgment; when the nation's pride is broken his anger will vanish, and his love will return like a refreshing dew.

The theme of an eschatological national salvation or End of Days is also much developed in postexilic prophetic literature. The realization of God's historic purpose will demand the restoration of the national existence in a life of peace and security, under a Davidic king as a mark of real continuity with the old Israel. The very face of nature will be transfigured by the presence of the Lord who renews all things.

For Jeremiah, the Covenant whose failure he had lamented will be replaced by a Covenant which will be new because made with a people renewed in heart and mind. God will be known directly, as Jeremiah knew him. He will write on men's hearts the Law those hearts refused when it was imposed from without. His forgiveness will remove for all time the effect of the sin which had alienated man from man, and man from God. "They shall all know me, from the least of them unto the greatest of them."

If the world as nature is understood as the sphere of God's sovereignty and the stage for man's labors and the working out of his destiny, that means that in the last resort nature is regarded as history rather than as nature. The real sphere where God rules is history: he makes his works known in the history of Israel. In its early stages, Hebrew thought did not think of Yahweh as the God of the world. But he came to be conceived as such in the teaching of the prophets. He was essentially righteous will, demanding righteousness from men. He could not, therefore, be confined to the limits of a single nation. By acting as judge in the history of Israel, he became Lord over other nations as well as over natural events, which were now made into a part of the natural process. The creation story in Genesis 1 is not just a piece of speculation, but the first chapter in history. Beginning with creation, the course of history moved forward through the age of the patriarchs to Israel's development into a nation under Moses and the giving of the Law on Mount Sinai. In this history, in which men knew they were involved, they saw the exercise of God's judgment extending over all nations.

History is a major theme of biblical literature. It is never content with brief annals or chronicles, but describes a continuous historical course from one generation to another. But it has no sense of historical laws working throughout the universe. History is not, as in Greek literature, the scientific study of the past as a means of finding out the eternal laws which govern all events. Rather, it looks toward the future, to a divinely appointed goal. The prophets call attention to God's favor and punishment in the past; they show how he is carrying out his purpose in the teeth of the rebellion of his people. They pass judgment on the present, and drive home to the people their responsibilities in face of the future.

Apart from chronicles, there is no history in the real sense among the nations of the East. The same was originally true of the Romans. Historiography in the proper sense of the word, not just its early beginnings, is actually to be found only in Greek and Hebrew literature. In both cases the writing of history was the direct outcome of historical experience—with the Greeks, their wars of liberation against the Persians; in

Israel, the victorious struggle against the Philistines and the conquest of the cities of Canaan.

But perhaps the most important point about Hebrew historiography is that the center of interest is not politics, as with the Greeks but, rather, the purpose of God and his moral demands. Thus there is no concern with history as a science, no interest in the forces immanently at work in it. Its real interest is in relating the course of history to its end. Hence the division of history into epochs and the reflection on their significance for the whole historical process; and finally, a preoccupation with eschatology as the clue to its meaning. Historiography is sustained by a sense of responsibility on the part of the present toward the past and its heritage, and toward the future whether it brings salvation or disaster. History is not, as for Thucydides, material for educating the statesman, but homiletics for the people, driving home to all their responsibility.

The ethical precepts of righteousness and morality (as in the Decalogue, for instance) are regarded as the commandments of God. As king and patron of justice, God requires absolute and unconditional obedience to the covenant demands of righteousness and justice. No distinction is drawn between moral and ceremonial law, both being of equal importance. In fact, there is more scrupulousness in fulfilling the latter when the former is neglected. The prophets protest against this view. For them—or at any rate for the earlier prophets—God demands only righteousness and justice, not the performance of the cultus.

True, the prophets did not succeed in abolishing the cultus. The outcome of their work was its centralization at Jerusalem, which brought to an end the Canaanite vegetation rites and the corruption of the worship of Yahweh. And in addition to this, theirs was an attempt to recover a unity between the cultus and the judicial and moral law. A partial solution was found in the reinterpretation of the ancient ceremonial observances. The keeping of the Sabbath, for instance, was given a moral motive. More important, however, was the transformation of popular worship into a demonstration of obedience toward God and an effective symbol of Israel's separation from the surrounding nations with the temptations of their paganism. Thus the later prophets ceased to attack the cultus and interpreted it as

obedience to a divine institution. According to them, what God really wants is radical obedience—or the "heart" of man (as seen in Isaiah).

The old condition laid down for the sacrificial victim, namely, that it should be entire and without blemish, is reapplied to the worshiper himself.

Two factors led to an increasing sense of immorality and sin. First, there were the experiences of misfortune and distress in which the devout saw the punishment of God. Second, there was the teaching of the prophets, with their insistence on the inadequacy of the cultus, which led to a refined sense of conscience. Man was driven more and more to take refuge in the forgiving grace of God and to supplicate for pardon.

In this sense repentance is demanded of man. Repentance is not just a change of mind, however. That would be only a subjective process, leaving man's relation with God unaffected. Repentance (as proposed by the prophets) means returning to God from the isolation of self-will. It means recognizing God as the judge in whose sight man is guilty, and whose forgiveness alone can restore him to the community. Repentance thus involves an acceptance of God's judgment as transmitted by the prophet. More than remorse, it is an explicit act of self-surrender, an acknowledgment of a life forfeited. Of course, this turning to God does involve a change of disposition, a resolve to do good and obey God's will in time to come. But there is no suggestion that this resolve in itself is able to avert the wrath of God. All man can do is to ask God's forgiveness and hope to receive it (cf. Hos. 14:1; Isa. 55:6).

Since for ancient Israel life was confined to this world, and the only future after death was the future of the people, God's forgiveness and grace were transferred to an eschatological future: "In those days and at that time, saith the Lord, the iniquity of Israel shall be sought for and there shall be none; and the sins of Judah, and they shall not be found: for I will pardon them whom I reserve" (Jer. 50:20).

4

The Redemption of History

The Torah is anchored in events which occurred at one point in time and space. If God, as the Jewish faith affirms, has entered into the course of human history, then all history must be related to those facts upon which Judaism is founded and must derive its significance from them. What Judaism claims is not only that these events are historically true, but also that they are *the* truths of all history, both the history which is past and the history which is yet to be. We are therefore committed to a Jewish philosophy of history. If the Jewish world-view is to be commended to the minds of our bewildered generation, bruised and stunned by the impacts of history, that enterprise cannot be evaded.

Yet it is extraordinarily hard to present the Jewish interpretation in any way which can seem convincing to the "climate of opinion" in our own day. The Jewish interpretation must cut across most of the assumptions of our contemporary milieu. The Jewish world-view cannot be constructed simply in terms of temporal process, or of what is called "historical evolution," since biblical events involve, *ex hypothesi,* an invasion from a supra-temporal order. Nor can it be presented in terms of philosophical idealism. For idealism, like Platonism (whose ghost has occasionally haunted our religion), cannot admit that the temporal event which is once-for-all, concrete and contingent, is other than incomplete and half-real—and these are events within the time process.

Here, indeed, is the paradox which lies at the heart of all Jewish thinking, because it lies at the heart of Judaism: the affirmation of Jewish faith declares that the events recorded in the Torah as occurring in the time-process are not drowned out in the relativities of history, but are determinative and unique. They cannot be explained in the light of other events, since there are none with which they can be compared; yet they are the explanation of all others. This is perhaps the central conviction of the Jewish faith and must control its understanding of history. There is nothing else like it in human speculation. This is its "scandal of particularity," and Judaism's contribution to philosophical thought. If Judaism is "a faith seeking redemption," it is a faith engaged in real time, and under obligation to take time seriously. In the Jewish world-view, redemption and history coalesce.

Within this unitarian view, the answer can be found to the crux of all philosophical enquiry—how the order of supersensual reality, absolute ethical values and a priori concepts of reason, can be brought into one coherent totality with the contingent world of time and change. Translated into the language of religion, this sounds less abstract and academic. For religion, the problem is to understand how God can be related to the world in such a way as not to be so transcendent or otherworldly that he can have no actual contact with it, nor so completely immanent or present within it as to be the prisoner of his own creation. Only a messianic faith can respond effectively to that question.

This is implicit in the Jewish world-view, though it is inevitably paradoxical, for it can never be stated in purely rational terms. Since the Jewish world-view must be presented to popular understanding in the symbols and images of religious myth, the Jewish interpretation is suggested rather than logically stated in that mysterious and baffling element comprised within the prophetic tradition which biblical scholars now call eschatology—the prophecies and traditions associated with the coming of the Messiah and the Day of the Lord.

Even before World War II, this material was too much for us. It was just frankly and flatly incommensurable with views that most Jews of the Diaspora then took for granted. One school of

critics, and loosely organized at that, found the traditional Jewish ideas of messianism so intoxicating that for them it alone came to seem authentic. The messianic strain in the prophetic books of the Bible was, with whatever violence to the facts, claimed as alone genuine and true to the outlook and teaching of Judaism and of the biblical Israelite community. This was exaggerated and one-sided; but it was less remote from the truth than the conclusions which most of us accepted.

The majority of us went to the other extreme. We found all this so crude and uncongenial to our modern Jewish minds—as indeed it probably is—that we wanted to cut loose from it altogether. Prophetic messianism was due, we insisted, to the "supernatural" background in the minds of those earliest and most primitive Jews. It was not much more than a *façon de parler,* something purely local and temporary, not a permanent factor in the Judaic message. We wanted, therefore, to "restate" all this in terms which were, admittedly, less challenging but were yet radically inconsistent with it. We used instead the substitute languages of moral gradualism and evolution with a religious fervor. What it all means permanently, we said, is that the truth and power of Torah ethics will, year by year, grow in range and influence, and the world will little by little become better.

The strength of this "liberal" interpretation was that—confronted, as it seemed to be, with the choice between ethics and redemption—its supporters refused to abandon the ethical content of Judaism. If that were really the choice, they chose rightly. But, as we can see now in the light of subsequent thought and experience, it was not. The alternatives as presented were misleading; and as exegesis, this will never do, for this was "local and temporary" with a vengeance. It is hardly too much to describe it as provincial. The liberal world-view was trying to fit the Torah outlook into the frame of its own suppositions; or, to put the same thing in another way, it was trying to superimpose the liberal philosophy of nineteenth-century progress upon the minds of the earliest Jewish writers.

The course of events, meanwhile, has overwhelmed this liberal interpretation. True, the last twenty years have seen the establishment of the State of Israel, when it had been assumed by many Jews that it was already a lost cause. That is a wholly legitimate appeal, and a cordial for drooping Jewish spirits. But there is another side to the picture. Some countries are now closed to Judaism, in others it is officially restricted, and in some behind the Iron Curtain the whole power of the state is ranged against it. Nor can anyone easily maintain that there is, or has been, a steady moral progress. There has been appalling moral retrogression. Crimes and cruelties which we took for granted that civilization had long left behind, are now so much everyday occurrences, and on so frightful a scale, that we hardly notice them. I do not see how any impartial survey could deny that during the last two decades, in the ancient homelands of our Patriarchs, the forces of evil have been gaining ground.

Thus Jews who still believe in Judaic-ethic gradualism are finding themselves with nothing left today beyond repeating a moral exhortation which degenerates into vague religious uplift. ("The world would be much nicer than it is if only people were nicer than they are.") But the drama of our history was not wrought out to support such watery sentiments. In this era in which we are living, we can now at least understand why Torah has always been proclaimed not so much in terms of ethical ideals, but in terms of historical redemption. Torah does not provide mere mottoes for ethical societies. It offers real faith for real people in a real, and often extremely dangerous, world. What is the use of ethical "ideals" in such a world as men know today, unless God had actually *done* something to stamp his seal and signature on history? That is what Torah's redemptive history means. It guarantees the victory of God's will and the reconciliation of history through him by whom all things were made—and that is to say, its ultimate redemption. Torah gives no true sanction to the creed of "progress."

The Torah does not appear to look forward through long vistas of orderly development broadening down to prosperity and peace. Rather, it seems to expect the exact contrary—that evil men will wax worse and worse, that there will be wars, famines, revolutions, increasing distress for Israel, an ever-mounting curve of catastrophe, till the redemptive age comes to pass and Zion is restored. In a sense, of course, it does not look "forward" at all, because its perspectives are violently foreshortened by expectations of imminent disaster. So far as it does begin to look forward, Utopia is certainly not on its horizon. And indeed, the whole idea of an "evolution" toward a perfection at some future time, ever receding into a further distance, is entirely alien to its thought. Torah understands history in terms of crisis, not in terms of gradual development; to a large extent, the lines are perpendicular, not horizontal. The crisis is in both judgment and deliverance, and every age is a crisis of the world.

The prophetic consciousness as exhibited in the prophets of Israel, is a variety of a general religious consciousness, involving an immediate fellowship of the prophet (as interpreter of God's will) with God; but both in the sphere of its exercise and in the form of its experience, it presents several phenomena which do not belong to the permanent essence of religious Judaism.

Though the prophets are conscious of being intermediaries between Yahweh and the nation of Israel, it is always as representatives of Yahweh, the national God of Israel—the God who had known that people alone of all the families of the earth (Amos 3)—that they speak the "word of Yahweh"; and the message they deliver in his name is addressed not to themselves personally, nor to each Israelite individually, but to the nation in its corporate capacity, conceived as an organic unity and often idealized as a moral person. In addition, the prophets of Israel appear to have been endowed with remarkable insight into the providential significance of the political events of their time. History being to the nation what experience is to the individual, it was only through his providential ordering of history that God could express his dealings with a nation, and only through the prophetic interpretation of providence that his mind could be truly known. In pre-exilic literary prophecy, the dissolution of this gracious relationship and the consequent destruction of the state are announced as a moral necessity brought about by the persistent disobedience of Israel and the inflexible righteousness of Yahweh. But this startling message of doom remains an interpretation of the divine purpose as participial, as a purpose *about to be* manifested in an imminent crisis of history.

The experience of the prophets contains a subconscious element, appearing chiefly in the form of the vision, which is not characteristic of what is commonly understood to be normal religious life. The prophetic vision is undoubtedly a creation of the subconscious mind, working uncontrolled by voluntary reflection and producing subjective images which have something of the vividness and reality of actual sense perception. Apparently the visions recorded by the prophets were actually experienced by them in a condition of comparative ecstasy, in which self-consciousness was not lost, although control of the visionary process was suspended.

Elijah is the true forerunner of the prophets, not only in the matter of Naboth's vineyard, but also in his return to Horeb to recover his inspiration and strength. The Rechabites (Jer. 35; II Kings 10) not only abjured viniculture and agriculture in general, but carried their nomadism to the point of continuing to dwell in tents. We can see the nomadic tradition very clearly in Amos, the first of the great series. In Puritan fashion, he denounces the luxury and "culture" of the northern kingdom, and its elaborate and excessive religiosity. He contrasts his own times with the days of the desert, when there were no such sacrifices and offerings in the worship of Yahweh, a distinction which may, it is suggested, be taken as expressive of a *relative* truth, in view of what was true about nomadic religion.

Though Isaiah belongs to a different social level than that of Amos, Micah, and Elijah, he is no less indignant at the treatment of the helpless. His scorn for Canaanite idolatry is matched only by his condemnation of ceremonial worship without morality. His own sense of the true attitude of man before the Holy One of Israel is shown in the account of his calling to prophecy.

But this attitude toward the externals of worship is most explicit and pronounced in Jeremiah (chap. 7). In the spirit of Amos, Jeremiah thinks of the nomadic period as one in which God gave no commandments concerning burnt offerings or sacrifices, which at least implies (but by no means fixes as a certainty) that the elaborate ritual ascribed to Moses in the Pentateuch was unknown to both those prophets. Also in the spirit of Amos, Jeremiah contrasts the luxurious dwelling of

Jehoiakim with the simpler life of his father, Josiah, whose glory was not in cedar paneling and vermillion paint, but in judging the cause of the poor. In relation to man, as in relation to God, the essentials of life are moral: this is the cardinal message of the prophets.

What, it may now be asked, is the relationship of these prophets, with their highly developed moral and religious teaching, to such "prophecy" as ascribed to Canaanite influence, e.g., that of the ecstatics encountered by Saul? One view may be that the canonical prophets are the direct descendants of these early *nebi'im,* and continue in greater or less degree their ecstatic and abnormal behavior. Another view may contrast the two classes: that the violent excitation usual in early prophecy had almost disappeared, that the prophet was conscious of being an independent individual person in the sense that his communion with God was a communion of two moral persons.

There is, however, far too much evidence of psychological abnormality for it to be explained away, even in Jeremiah, whose prophetic consciousness comes nearest to this moral definition. He was controlled from without and, as it seemed to him, irrationally; he saw strange visions; he had to wait ten days on one occasion for the desired word of Yahweh. There seems to have been no difference between the *forms* of "false" prophecy and the true; the difference was in the moral and religious quality of the message, and Jeremiah was unable *at the time* to denounce as false the prophecy of Hananiah, contradicting his own. The element of important truth in those views which minimize or deny the "ecstatic" element is that in the canonical prophets this element was thrust from the center to the circumference of their teaching. Something of the old forms remained theirs, and without these forms they would not have recognized themselves or have been recognized by others as divinely commissioned prophets. But they had risen far above the former levels; they were individuals emboldened to challenge the nation or its kings, not bands of professional dervishes echoing the royal policy. This is well brought out in the contrast of one of their forerunners, Micaiah, with the four hundred court prophets of Ahab (I Kings).

Furthermore, the fact that Israel lay in the corridor between the great empires of the Near East, those of Egypt and Mesopotamia, had consequences as important for religion as for the realm of politics. Israel's checkered history brought great opportunities for religion to develop through the very demands made by it, for the prophets of Israel had to face a challenge as severe as any people could be called to meet.

It is important to see how this prophetic faith works out in practice when it is challenged by the new demands of history. Isaiah is, perhaps, the clearest example of it. History, he says, is under the control of God. Since his purpose cannot fail, there will be a "righteous remnant," even though the nation as a whole be condemned. But that righteous remnant will need a local habitation, and so Zion will stand, whatever the Assyrians may do. Isaiah is pre-eminently the prophet of faith, and his faith makes its fact by a resolute reinterpretation of the bare event, as well as by an unbroken confidence in Israel's authentic future.

It is significant of the variety of such interpretations of history that Isaiah's contemporary, Micah, proclaimed the downfall of Jerusalem at that very crisis. The overthrow of Israel constantly asserted by the pre-exilic prophets was not, indeed, a merely political inference, but neither was it a merely moral inference. It was a unity intuitively perceived, yet one that can be analyzed by us into these two lines of approach, since the prophets never taught without reference to, and often prompting from, contemporary events, though their teaching can never be resolved into shrewd political calculation.

To be sure, the religion of the eighth-century B.C.E. prophets was driven underground during the pagan reaction of Manasseh's long reign, but it reappeared in the book of Deuteronomy, of which the central portion was the program of Josiah's reformation in 621 B.C.E. In these codes one may observe the influence of the prophets, especially of Hosea. In both the humanitarian morality and the centralization of worship and festivals at Jerusalem in order to secure their purification and adequate control. Jeremiah was a contemporary of this reformation and seems at first to have supported it. If so, the resultant emphasis on the temple, as though this guaranteed security, subsequently alienated him. It was inevitable that the reform, however necessary a compromise between prophetic and priestly interests, should work out in favor of those who represented the institutional side of religion. Through Jeremiah's own experience of the revelation of God to the inner man, he was led to the conviction that the only cure for social and religious ills must be found in a "new covenant," in strong and explicit contrast with such an externally expressed covenant as Deuteronomy had set forth. He had discovered that the true Israelite, as well as his God could do without a temple, and therefore he could contemplate the overthrow of the state without fear, though with profound sympathy with those who would suffer through it.

Here for us is the innermost truth of Jewish history: the world is always under God's judgment and is always being redeemed by his power. Thus every time is a time of the end. The Torah does, undeniably, look forward to a consummation in history—as it must, if history belongs to God and his purpose is operative in it. Yet that "end" is also always present. For the Day of the Lord is a present reality—not a far-off, divine event; and the kingdom of the Lord is ever pressing in on this historical order of time and change—always here, always yet to come.

It would be hard to find anything less congruous with the modern creeds of secular Futurism than this eschatological approach to history. Whether in their liberal or their Marxist form, they are "heresies" of Judaism, with God and Torah cut out of it. They could only have grown up against a Christian background. The original sources of their inspiration were the biblical evaluations of history as the arena of a divine purpose moving toward an end and a climax, and the Christian expectation of their Lord's coming and of an eternal hope for all men. It is only on Christian soil that the "golden age" is envisaged as still ahead; and without that bracing hope and expectation, man's historical task has no incentive for them. This secular hope with its Christian roots, expressed by many contemporary Jews, withers under the blasts of disappointment and sinks into historical determinism, or else into cynicism and despair.

In the ancient world, the mystery-religions offered a

privileged and private exit by which the initiated could escape from the challenge and frustrations of history, leaving the world unredeemed behind them. It would not be hard to convert men today to a modernized mystery-religion, Buddhist or theosophical in tendency. Escapist mysticism is alluring. Even Jews have at times succumbed to it, especially when the historical situation seemed to deny Jewish opportunity. The more insensitive the world becomes to the recognition of religious values, the more seductive will the temptation be. But this is moral and spiritual defeatism. What we need is a faith which is not at the mercy of circumstances or the vicissitudes of this mortal life—a hope that is not merely wishful thinking, and a faith re-established in Torah, reaching out beyond these years of time to an inheritance which is incorruptible. Such is the eternal hope of Judaism.

Yet Judaism is not "optimistic." The authentic Jewish hope gives no encouragement to any kind of secular Utopianism. Judaism takes a tragic view of history. (Marxism is a great deal nearer to it than any form of liberal evolutionism and is for that reason a far more dangerous rival.) If, as is probable, we must now look forward to a period of radical insecurity haunted by constant danger and anxiety, that should be no shock to the thought or to the faith of Jews. It is what we are schooled to expect, both by our reading of Torah and by the Jewish philosophy of history.

5

The Higher Anthropomorphism

I anticipate that not a few of those who read this book will be conscious of a growing misgiving that they are being stealthily decoyed into an untenable anthropomorphism, into a reversion to the standpoint of a prescientific and prephilosophic age when man made God in his own image. By the simple savage or by half-civilized man, this may be done with a good conscience, but we are the heirs of all the ages; so intellectually, at least, we are obliged to be somewhat more respectable.

This particular misgiving is one which, if I am at liberty to quote my own experience, I may say that I have lived through and lived down. For the last century and more, educated men—in acute reaction against the anthropomorphic theism of secular Judaism—in speaking of the Ultimate Being have instinctively preferred to use words of an impersonal connotation, such as the Supreme Being, the Absolute, the All-pervading, the Veiled Being, and the like. But in philosophy, as in politics, reaction against one extreme may easily result in another just as bad or, perhaps, even worse. The category of personality is not only religiously the most inspiring that we can apply to the power behind the universe, it is also intellectually the least inadequate. In an earlier period of history, a crude anthropomorphism was a danger to be feared; in our age, what the philosopher of religion and the rabbi want is the courage to advance more confidently toward what, abandoning all shamefacedness, I will call the higher anthropomorphism.

So long as materialism seemed to the majority of scientists to give an adequate account of the phenomena of life, consciousness could only be regarded as an epiphenomenon—a curious and useless shadow cast by the solid substance of reality. But, once we are driven by further observation of the facts of organic life—including, of course, those studied by psychology—to postulate something like a life-force behind the universe, the case is altered. Those "bits" of individuals, those aspects of the living mind which the generalizations of physical science are bound to leave out of their purview, and also that inexplicable "individual" ego which even psychology cannot include, must somehow or other be brought back upon the ledger before the final accounts are passed. The subtler qualities of life not only may but must be brought into consideration. Thought, feeling, the sense of value—things which cannot be seen, measured, or counted—and that psychic entity we call individuality, may well turn out to be just those elements that will supply a key to the understanding of the whole. It is not merely legitimate to bring these things in, it is illegitimate to leave them out.

For Judaism to reach a true conception of reality, we must combine in a single comprehensive scheme all that can be discovered along each of two different ways of knowledge. First comes the investigation of the material universe by the methods of pure science. Second, there must be carefully controlled inference as to the nature and quality of that indwelling creative life which is partially expressed in all living organisms. In man that life finds expression in a more intense, and therefore probably a more representative, form; and this is also a form of which we have direct knowledge in our own inner experience.

To use this knowledge to interpret creative life is, I frankly admit, in effect to *personify* the power behind things. But personification, provided it is always checked and controlled by the results of scientific observation, is not only a legitimate mode of conception, it is a necessary one. If I am to interpret any life other than human, I must, to however limited an extent and with whatever degree of qualification and hesitation, use my own inner experience as a key; that is, I must "personify" it. If I affirm of a dog that he is affectionate, frightened, ill-tempered, or disappointed, I speak of the dog as if it were a person. But the personality which I thus ascribe to the dog must be understood to have, as it were, a large minus quantity appended. If I attribute such qualities to a rabbit, I am still implicitly ascribing to it personality, but with an increase in the appended minus quantity. But, instead of looking downward, I may look up; I may venture to use my own experience of the inner quality of life to interpret the quality of the universal life. Then I am ascribing personality to it; but in that case, it is with a large plus.

This brings us up against a difficulty. Granted that it is admissible to ascribe personality to the power behind the universe, provided that conception be used with a meaning indefinitely enlarged—must not that enlargement be so enormous as to dwarf to the point of insignificance the original meaning of the term "person"? Granted that it may be more appropriate to speak of that power as "He" than as "It," yet if He and It are both conceived as infinite, is there, for our poor human intellects, any practical difference between them? Have not both pronouns lost all real meaning?

This objection is crushing—until we realize that the essence of personality and of its inward life does not consist in quantity but in quality. A man's passion for his ladylove takes up no more room in space than his affection for his great-aunt; the difference is one of intensity and quality, not of size. The difference between the kind of disapprobation with which a fashionable undergraduate regards a man who wears the wrong tie and that with which Jeremiah viewed the inhabitants of ancient Israel is a difference which may be described as "worldwide"—but that does not imply that it is one to which the diameter of the earth is in the smallest degree relevant. Once we grasp the point that personality and its characteristics are a matter of quality, not of quantity, we can brave that "astronomical intimidation" to which otherwise from the mere size of the material universe we might succumb. If the essence of personality had anything at all to do either with size or with capacity to exert foot-pounds of physical force, any analogies or inferences from human to divine personality would be ridiculous. But when the Psalms, for instance, maintain that the quality of love as manifested in the personality of Israel may be an adequate representation of a quality inherent in the Divine, that contention, whether we accept it or not, is as least not inherently absurd.

To personify the power behind things is not, as so many fear, a "pathetic illusion"; it is a necessity of thought. It is sometimes said that philosophy demands an impersonal Absolute, religion a personal God. Nothing could be further from the truth. Unless the argument outlined above is wholly fallacious, any philosophy which does not conceive the Infinite as in some sense concretely personal is intellectually blind at one essential point. I assert that individuality is the synthetic focus of the living organism, and that in the ascending scale of evolution, individuality and freedom increase as life reveals itself in forms ever more intense and more highly organized. Analogy suggests that this principle applies also to the life in the universe. The universe is a coherent system–otherwise science could not interpret it in terms of law–and it is the expression of a living power; then is it not of living organisms the most highly organized of all? Unless we are to conceive of that life as less vital than our own, we must ascribe to it that element in personality which makes it a focus of synthetic activity. We must not think of it as an "ocean of life," or even as "a stream of consciousness," but as a closely knit, highly centralized, self-consistent, fully self-conscious, eternally creative unity. That is, we must not regard the ultimate reality as merely in a vague way personal; we must ascribe to it what, for want of a richer word, we can only call individuality. Indeed, I would go so far as to maintain that to individualize the Deity by the use of a proper name like *Yahweh* is, up to a point, philosophically more sound than to think of him exclusively in abstract impersonal terms like the Ineffable or the Absolute.

But though to personify the power behind things is a necessity, it is a dangerous necessity. Man cannot be trusted to make God in his own image. Pass in review all the things that man has imagined his Deity to demand or to approve: human sacrifice, temple prostitution, grotesque asceticism, the rack and the stake, not to mention the endless routine of senseless ritual and trivial superstition. *Tantum religio potuit suadere malorum!* A religion which personifies unworthily the power behind things will do far more to retard than to advance the highest welfare of the race. That is why one epoch in human progress vis-à-vis human consciousness dates from the suggestion, perhaps first made by Moses, that instead of picturing God in their own image, or in the image traditional in a particular community, men should picture him in the image of Torah. Historic Judaism has never quite risen to this conception. Hitherto it has always compromised; its teachers have lacked, it seems to me, the insight or the courage to reject out and out certain elements in the conception of God derived from earlier beliefs. But insofar as Judaism has risen to its heritage and has conceived of God in terms of Torah, it has put before the world a personification of the Divine which at least is not unworthy.

To all this there is an objection, raised less by the professional philosopher than by the average educated man. Personality in human experience is associated with limitation, idiosyncrasy, and caprice. The power behind things, whatever else it may be, is not such: Does it not, above all manifest itself in a reign of law? The reign of law seems incompatible with the idea that the power of whose activity it is the expression is one to which the term "personal" can properly be applied; for in the popular notion, the essence of personality seems to be freedom to change one's mind or vary one's conduct. But human beings chop and change about, not because they are persons, but because they are persons subject to infirmity of purpose, or liable to be confronted with unforeseen or unforeseeable emergencies—and these are negative conditions of human life, not positive qualities of personality as such. If we speak of the power behind things as personal, we must attribute to it a steadiness of purpose and a range of knowledge infinitely transcending ours. Should we not then expect its activities to function in a way calculable and consistent, which to us must appear as necessary and unalterable laws: "God is not a man that he should lie, neither the son of man that he should repent." We are apt to forget that no conception and therefore no word which we can apply to God can be really appropriate. Ideas, and the words in which we express them, derive what meaning they have from things and conditions of which we have experience. What idea or word appropriate to our limited experience could be adequate to describe the Infinite? But, unless the whole argument of this book is fallacious, personality is much the least inadequate. The idea of personality is, as it were, the window through which we look out upon the limitless beyond; it is the smoked glass through which alone we can behold the sun.

Some thinkers would prefer to use the word "supra-personal"; if this were to become current coin, it might do well enough. Still, in my judgment, "personal" is really the better, because the safer, word. It is at least full of concrete meaning (incidentally, it does justice to the testimony of religious experience) and it can be used without danger of intellectual error because no educated person is likely to forget that in speaking of God as personal we are expanding the idea of personality to meet this special case. On the other hand, if we refuse to call God personal, and conscientiously use words like "supra-personal," we are pretty certain to end by thinking of him as impersonal. Thought in the last resort is controlled by imagination, and it does matter whether the word we use seems to stand for he or it; and to the imagination, "supra-personal" inclines to stand for it. It is, I believe, better to do a slight violence to language than to impoverish thought; it is preferable to expand the idea of personality rather than to contract our idea of God. To think or to speak of the Infinite in abstract and impersonal terms is unconsciously to liken him to forces lower, poorer, and less full of vitality than ourselves, such as the electric current or the life principle in a tree. To say that God is "personal but something more," is to say that the creative principle must be higher than the highest, richer than the richest, more full of life than the most alive of all things It has produced—and that surely is merely common sense.

Since the world and its component elements are not affections of the Divine Substance and inherent in it but, rather, are altogether distinct from it, pantheism is repugnant to reason. This assertion is directed against the pantheists who maintain that the assemblage of things which we call the world is really the Divine Absolute Being under various aspects; these aspects they are pleased to call sometimes moments, sometimes determinations, sometimes modes.

I am not here concerned with the semipantheistic theories of emanation, according to which living creatures are particles separated from the Divine Substance. My proposition is directed against pantheism in its so-called perfect form. I shall consider it only in its most general outlines, as it manifests itself in some fundamental theorems common to the well-known pantheistic systems of Spinoza, Fichte, Schelling, and Hegel. These authors, though starting from very different principles, agree with one another in these two assertions:

I. Properly speaking, there exists only one Being. This one Being is called Substance by Spinoza, the Pure Ego by Fichte, the Absolute by Schelling, the Logical Concept by Hegel.

II. The one Being evolves itself by a necessity of fate into forms of Being, diverse from, and opposed to, one another, inasmuch as they are so many several determinations under which the first Being manifests itself under all these diverse determinations.

Against these assertions, I say that the "attributes" of God when compared to our external and internal experience, forbid us to admit that the same being is really common to God and to the things of this world. God is one undivided Being, in no way composed of parts; he unites all perfections in the identity of his unchangeable existence. On the other hand, external and internal experience bear witness to the fact that the world round about us, and human beings themselves, form not really one undivided substance, but many separate individuals, each complete in its own being, differing from, and not seldom opposed to, another in natural or voluntary tendencies.

Is it not ridiculous to say that a cat is the same real being with the mouse she devours, and with the dog that worries her, and that cat and dog alike are the same being with the master who with his whip restores peace between them? Is it not absurd to maintain that the criminal to be hanged is really the same being with the judge who pronounces sentence of death against him, and with the executioner who carries out this sentence? And who can accept the statement that the atheist is substantially the same being with God, whose existence he denies and whose name he blasphemes?

Moreover, experience tells us that there is nothing in the

material world known to man which is not either composed of parts or a part itself; and that, consequently, nothing is complete and perfect in its simplicity. How then can this world be really one being with God, with the Being who is in the highest degree and in a truly objective way, simple? Finally, reason based upon experience teaches us that the purely corporeal world lacks altogether the faculties of understanding and free will, and that these faculties, even in the most gifted of the human race, are in a state of imperfection and perfectibility. It is, therefore, absolutely impossible that either the corporeal or the spiritual world known to men should be one with God who is infinitely perfect, and therefore under all aspects without defect, and incapable of evolving new perfections or new modes of perfection in his own Being.

The evolution of the Deity, as stated by the pantheists, is not only opposed to God's attributes, but also involves a contradiction. There is nothing by which God's "evolution" could be caused but the internal activity of God the Creator. Now, an activity by which the Creator should produce in itself what it does not already possess is inconceivable. Such production would result in effects contained in their total cause neither formally nor eminently; that is to say, neither in the same way in which they exist when produced, nor in a higher way more than equivalent to the existence of them all. The total cause of the determinations of Being into which the pantheistic Deity evolves itself, is supposed to be this Deity itself, without the determinations to be evolved. For these cannot be in that Deity formally, before their evolution takes place; otherwise there would be no evolution. Nor can they be said to exist in it eminently, before they are formally actuated; because on this supposition the first Being, so far from tending by its evolution to unfold its own essence, as pantheists would have it, would tend, rather, to corrupt that essence and to make a monster of it. Indeed, as Hegel says: "What kind of an Absolute Being is that which does not contain in itself all that is actual?"

Consequently, on the pantheistic hypothesis, the Creator as First Cause is less perfect before it determines itself than it becomes by such determination: and yet this lower perfection suffices to effect the determination and raise it to a more perfect state. In other words, it is in itself the total cause of successive advancements in perfection, without previously possessing those superadded perfections either formally or eminently. Thus the pantheistic God continually violates the inviolable principle of causality; and either the principle of causality or pantheism must go.

Finally, what becomes of morality in the pantheistic hypothesis? Is there still room for a distinction between actions really good and really bad? If pantheism is true, all actions are good. The coward and the hero, the miser and the philanthropist, the tyrant and the martyr, all are deserving of praise; for they all do what the supreme law, which rules the evolution of the Absolute, inexorably demands: their actions are nothing but a manifestation of the pantheistic God as he necessarily must be according to a law of fate inherent in his nature. Spinoza does not seem to shrink from a barefaced acceptance of this necessary inference from his pantheistic system. Thus, for instance, he expresses himself in his *Ethics* to the effect that no action considered in itself is either good or bad—an assertion he bases upon this practical maxim: "To enjoy ourselves insofar as that may be done short of satiety or disgust—for here excess were no enjoyment—is true wisdom."

According to the theory expressed in Spinoza's *Ethics,* there is only one substance, unproduced and infinite—God. Besides God, no substance can exist or be conceived to exist; consequently, whatever is, is in God; it is a mode or affection of the Divine Nature. God is not the transient or external cause of all things but, rather, their immanent cause; they are all determined by the necessity of the Divine Nature to exist and to act in a certain definite manner. Hence it follows that so-called freedom of will is a chimera, and that things could have been produced in no other way or order than as they have been produced.

These are the leading tenets of the thirty-six propositions, in which Spinoza, in the first part of his *Ethics,* explains his views about the primary cause of all things. From my general refutation of pantheism given above, it is evident that these propositions contradict external and internal experience, and contain a virtual denial of the first principles both of speculative and of practical reason. Yet they are worked out with a show of exactness which has captivated, while it has imposed upon, many minds. It becomes, therefore, worthwhile to deal with them in some measure. I shall, however, confine myself to the one underlying fallacy on which the entire system is based. This is Spinoza's misuse of his ambiguous definition of substance, which I shall examine briefly, and which in spite of the general unpopularity of his system, had led the way to the German pantheists Fichte and Hegel and to more modern forms of monism.

Spinoza rests his proof that God is the only possible substance on the proposition that one substance cannot be produced by another substance, which is a virtual assertion of pantheism. This proposition is proved by a series of previous propositions, all of which are based on the definition of substance with which he starts. Substance is defined by Spinoza as "that which is in itself and conceived by itself alone, that is to say, that of which the concept can be formed without involving any other concept."

This definition is patently ambiguous, and in order to make sure whether Spinoza's sixth proposition is really implicitly contained in it, we must inquire into the different ways in which the definition may be understood. Its meaning depends upon the interpretation of the phrase "that which is in itself and is conceived by itself." This may signify (1) a complete individual, physical being, as distinguised from its natural properties and accidental modifications; it may also signify (2) a self-existing being, a being under all aspects independent of any other being, whether as an underlying subject in which it inheres, or as a cause from which it proceeds. On the first interpretation, Spinoza's definition of substance is almost identical with the Scholastic definition; on the second, his definition is not applicable to any but the first Being, the Divine Essence, and as this Essence cannot be multiplied, Spinoza's Proposition VI, "One substance cannot produce another substance," follows from it, and this involves pantheism.

Yet the absurdity of pantheistic monism should illustrate fully that nobody can interpret substance in the second meaning of Spinoza's definition without committing himself to sheer nonsense. As to the steps of reasoning by which Spinoza reaches his famous Proposition VI, it will be sufficient to remark upon the first. His Proposition I runs thus: "Substance is prior in nature to its affections." In proof of it, he says nothing but that it follows from his definitions of substance and mode. I have said enough about the former. The latter is as follows: "By mode I understand an affection of substance or that which is in something else by which also it is apprehended." This may signify a substantial principle imparting to the whole its specific character, or a natural property really distinct from the being of which it is predicated, or an accidental modification of a being. Thus the soul of a dog is in the matter of its body as a specifying principle: the faculty of understanding, considered in its operations, is in the human soul as a natural property really distinct from the soul; and the derangement of mind is in the anti-Semite as an accidental modification.

If, then, we take Spinoza's definition of substance in the first of the two senses given above, and his definition of mode in the first of the three senses just explained, his first proposition is false. It is not true, for instance, that a dog is prior in nature to the specifying nature called his soul. Taking the same interpretation of the definition of substance along with the second and third interpretations of the definition of mode, we find the first proposition to be evidently true; for it is undeniable that natural properties and accidental modifications of a particular being cannot be conceived, except as following the existence of that being. Insofar as they do not follow its existence in the order of time, they at least follow it in the order of nature, that is to say, their existence cannot be conceived but on the supposition that the being exist of which they are predicated.

Finally, if we take Spinoza's definition of substance in the second sense given above, and his definition of mode in any of the three senses explained, it appears at once that his first proposition is altogether false. If God is physically and metaphysically simple, he is therefore not a substance like matter, which can be raised to diverse substantial degrees by the reception of diverse specifying. Nor are there in him natural properties to be conceived as something under certain aspects really distinct from his essence, and following that essence, in the way that an act of our understanding is really distinct from, and follows, the essence of the soul. Much less can God be the subject of merely accidental modifications.

But in what sense does Spinoza take his two definitions? Explicitly he does not tell us. Yet in the arguments by which he supports his subsequent propositions, there is not any force unless substance be taken in the third sense suggested. Hence it is evident that in Spinoza's very first proposition are hidden two false suppositions, the one that substance is synonymous with self-existence, the other that self-existence is changeable.

The centrality of the spirit in Judaism has to be understood not as the existence of a central point or force surrounded by nonspiritual layers, but as a penetrating operative reality which determines the character Jewish activity in all its layers. No Jewish activity is nonspiritual. Jews neither eat nor make love merely as animals. Nor, of course, are the political and economic activities of a Jew's existence entirely nonspiritual. Even his nonspiritual theories of existence are self-disproved when applied to himself.

The spirit-centered structure of Judaism is the ground both of the proper place of each activity and of the misplacement of one or more of them. The centrality of the spirit in Jews has thus a dual and ambivalent force. It is a fact of a Jew's existence and belongs to him by creation; all his doings are those of a being in whom the spiritual center is involved with nonspiritual reality and permeates it. In another sense, the spirit—because it is *neshamah* and not nature—can deny its centrality and eject itself somewhere else, and the particular activity into which it is injected is treated as the Jewish *centrum.* Recent events and a good deal of older history provide the story of man's spiritual fixation upon his political, his technical, or his trading activities, his class or his race. This is the sociological expression of egocentricity, which is precisely the opposite of the centrality of the spirit as the basic fact of Jewish existence. The ego, which is the spirit becoming an object to itself, identifies itself with activities and relationships and falsifies them. This is the *psychikos* man of Pauline Christianity, *le moi haïssable* of Pascal. In Judaism, however, what is uncovered is the possibility of the removal of the ego from individuality. The spirit, turned inside-in, now looks outward with love and righteousness instead of curling in on itself. The spirit recovers its centrality, its freedom, because it is open inward to God.

A Jew finds God speaking through him about his relationships and activities. The centrality of his spirit consists in its being the outpost in the world of the free, creative activity of God; it shares in a delegated sense in the transcendent quality of *ha-Shem.* And because the Jew belongs by his nature to the transcendent *ha-Shem,* when a Jew violates in any level of his consciousness that essential dependence upon ("hanging from") God, then the human function onto which the spirit of a Jew is projected is exalted into the place of God. Then the authority of Torah and the proper "natural" place of *halakhah* is threatened—and life disintegrates into a conflict between functional egoisms. Periods of rationalism, for instance, where human life is supposed to be directed toward its fulfillment by reason only, are always reacted against by an uprush of emotional and romantic forces. When the state claims what only God may claim, the proper place not only of politics but of the arts and industries is denied. The natural order is violated.

So the centrality of the spirit in Judaism has a sociological as well as a personal force. In the personal life, the true centrality cannot be recovered by the individual man through his own will alone; he must immerse his self in the divine action operating upon and through him, a process begun and carried through by the spiritual culture we call the practice of *halakhah.* So also, the centrality of spirit in its sociological force cannot be recovered by moral desire alone, but requires that this desire be sustained and that real will be formed out of it by a social order that provides a habitat for the soul. In other words, living becomes ex-centric not only when the Jewish spirit, in stark idolatry, deifies one of its powers, such as that of reason, politics, sex, or money; but also and equally when, however fine its intentions, it exercises any of these powers on a plane which does not belong to it.

The freedom of the Jew is won by that surrender to *ha-Shem* which life in Torah makes possible. It is the freedom in which he is delivered from feeling inwardly crushed by being involved in the social disorder in which he lives. He accepts that as a fact of his existence and can then take up an attitude which is capable of changing the disorder in an objectively right way. But he knows that short of the eschatological Day of the Lord, that inner freedom is always being lost unless he uses its initial gifts to build up a culture of the spirit by prayer and inwardness and discipline, and by faithfulness to Torah. He knows that he obtained this freedom only because God knows that he could do nothing to gain it.

So the Jew who knows what his redemption means, knows also when he turns to the organized public life of man that the natural order of human life, though in no sense commensurate with the Freedom of the Jew, is nevertheless something necessary for the life of all men. Necessary, not only because it is a noumenal reality which tugs at him all the time; he therefore suffers in the alienation because it is never a complete alienation. The Jewish believer wants this conflict lessened. For one thing, he is himself involved in it, though his spiritual freedom prevents his being overwhelmed by it; he knows the crucial inner struggle of surrender that is the cost of holding onto this freedom. But for a deeper reason, he wants the conflict lessened for all men and its significance elucidated.

A society which reflected in its culture something of a natural order would not ensure the redemption of a single Jew, but it might free that Jew's mind from confusion and his will from frustrations which come from mistaking a conflict of social purpose for a defect in the nature of things or for the effects of conscious human egoism. Where he failed, the failure would be more distinctly a moral failure. No such society exists, but societies are comparable by the extent to which they approach a natural order in all or some of their relationships, or depart from it.

A Jew is never free from the tug of the natural order in his being, however contradicted it is in his personal action and the false structure of his societies. But the double fact that it holds him and that he also contradicts it is evidence that his natural life is not a self-contained whole. It stands in a dependent relation to the transcendent reality of *ha-Shem*.

Because of this, he has the freedom to contravene his own

nature by a denial of his dependence. This is possible only by the freedom in it by God, who is God not only "by nature" but also by speaking to us through Torah. This cannot be expressed speculatively, but only by that mythological mode of the book of Genesis which posits a relationship to God beyond that of the human nature created by the Creator, namely, a relationship of responsible obedience and righteousness explicit in the Creator's Covenant with Israel.

Yet, though the contradiction violates it, it does not destroy the pull of the Creator's true nature. If God's existence consisted only in God's nature, then the violation of God's nature would leave no room for the pull back which all the time operates upon him.

The relation of Torah to the idea of a natural order may now be summarized. Torah is the offer of redemptive knowledge from the transcendent God who creates, who is present to and loves the man who in the immanent order toils for the good. Because God is transcendent as well as immanent in history, man can violate the conditions of his nature by denying the dependence of his existence upon something over and above his nature, namely, God. Because this dependent link continues to exist even when it is denied, man's natural existence, even in his alienation, shows this pulling back operating upon him. One is his elaboration of morality and law to prevent human sinfulness from destroying human existence. Positive law is at the same time the consequence of man's alienation from his true nature and also an expression of its continued operative power. It tells us that he is never merely the creature of nature and history but is held by his link with the transcendent reality.

The other fact is the action and reaction of man's dominant ideas about himself. A culture which gives central place to one activity or faculty of human life is displaced by one which appears to correct it and to be more "natural" to man. His nature never allows him collectively to remain "ex-centric" but in time pulls it over to another order, though this revolutionary process in the immanent order never finds equilibrium. Insofar as a generation is aware of the moving forces which are at work and the transcendent origin of what it is seeking, it can at least make for a relatively happier and more stable culture. And when, because of human pretensions, this culture is, as it must be, superseded in its turn, the subsequent transition is far more likely to be positive and human than our recent blind and destructive cataclysms have been.

The natural order of human life is therefore transcendent, in that it is essentially dependent upon God although he is wholly distinct from it; it is noumenal, in that its pattern is never a phenomenon to be observed, but its true meaning can be apprehended only by human intelligence; it is eschatological, in that it reaches its fulfillment only in God's final perfection of history. That natural order affects the phenomena of human cultures but it is never embodied totally in any of them. Men are led to cynical opportunism or impotent relativism when this fact of the natural order is denied; they are led to Utopian illusions and ideological tyrannies when it is assumed to be immanent in one set of social purposes and in the group of men who put these purposes into practice. The natural order exists as a norm and an operative force in man as such. The conscious task of any generation of Jews is to discover and to work with it. This necessarily takes the form of correcting the ways in which it has been violated in the previous period.

6

Rationalism, Prediction, and the Problem of Faith

"The scientific and technical world of modern man is the result of his daring enterprise, knowledge without love. Such knowledge is in itself neither good nor bad. Its worth depends on what power it serves. Its ideal has been to remain free of any power." I quote these words by the physicist Carl von Weizsäcker because they set the key for my discussion of the relationship between the rationalist and the faithful Jew. They emphasize very strongly that the professional relationship of the rationalist to his subject matter is a dispassionate, impersonal relationship; and I suggest that if we want to give this relationship a name we could call it that of the "observer-predictor." By "predictor," of course, I do not mean "fortune-teller" or "prophet" but "calculator"—essentially the observer who wishes to predict by calculations from what he observes—and I use this term to distinguish this relationship from two others.

Very roughly, we can think of three grades of relationship: first, the relationship of *dialogue,* at the level of person with person; second an observer relationship which is not one of impersonal detachment; it is what you might call the relationship of *observer-participant.* For example, think of a father watching the first steps of his small son. He is an observer, but he is not detached. At the sight of his son's tumbles, his reaction is not to predict the path which the child's body will take but to leap forward to catch him. He is an observer-participant: he still acts and feels part of the situation he is observing. And so both of these can be distinguished from the third relationship of *observer-predictor* in which the aim of the scientist is to withdraw from the situation as far as possible. He wants to reduce his participation to the minimum. In fact, he wants essentially to answer the question, "What would the situation be like without me?"

This element of withdrawn detachment is necessary for one very good reason, quite a technical one, which has only recently been explicitly worked out. Karl Popper is one of those who has brought out some of its implications. The point is this: if you have a predicting, calculating mechanism or human being, such a predicting mechanism cannot possibly predict exactly the future of any system which includes itself. The reason is that if you try to make it allow for the effect of its predictions on the system, it needs to know the prediction before it can calculate what effect this will have, and you simply set it chasing its own tail. It is a point that we will come back to later on in this chapter, but I want to emphasize it right at the beginning, because it is the technical reason for the absolute necessity of detachment, of withdrawal from the situation, on the part of the scientist.

Now of course, by saying this I do not mean that the scientist as a Jew cannot combine other attitudes with that of the observer-predictor. An astronomer who is a religious man may no doubt often be moved to worship as he looks for the first time on some new galaxy; but when he comes to measure its diameter, he measures it in just the same way as anybody else. We do not measure lengths piously; the idea makes no sense.

Nor do I want to deny that in scientific discovery there is a large element of nondeductive, creative thinking which is possible only through an imaginative response by the thinker, whether Jew or not, and which cannot happen if his attitude is one of complete detachment. To attempt to become the perfect machine in relation even to scientific subject-matter, is to become scientifically sterile. One could carry on routine scientific operations quite well, but inventive scientific thinking would become impossible.

My immediate concern is, roughly, with what the scientist is professionally allowed to say about his subject-matter, when he has cleared away the scaffolding of all these other rather logically disreputable operations of imaginative interaction which have enabled him to reach his conclusion. It may be that scientists use the most irrational procedures in thinking up new hypotheses, but when they come to write a paper all this must be cleared away, and the official relationship becomes that of the dispassionate observer-predictor.

In setting up this relationship of observer-predictor, then, there are two main problems. The first is the problem of withdrawing sufficiently from the situation while still remaining closely enough coupled to it to get information from it. This is, of course, a matter of compromise. The scientist requires something to happen (visibly, or detectably in some other way) in order that he can say something about the system he is observing; and for something to happen in his observing equipment, energy must pass to it from the system he is observing. So he must interact with the situation; but his problem is to interact with it as little as possible, so as to be able to make a description of what it would have been like if he had not interacted.

The first problem, then, is that of withdrawal, of reducing participation to the minimum. The second problem is one of defining a *language,* a connected set of ideas suitable for the detached viewpoint that he has chosen.

I want to illustrate these two problems and the ways in which they are met in two fields where especially interesting features stand out. The first field is the study of atomic events—very small-scale events; and the second is the scientific study of man himself—if you like, meeting oneself as the scientist sees one.

The Study of Atomic Events

Coming first to the study of atomic events, this is a field of very tiny energies, and it is almost a commonplace with us now that in order to extract sufficient energy from such a tiny thing as the atom, in order to be able to say something about what is happening in it, one disturbs it to an extent which is not negligible. If we are observing a billiard ball, then you might think that in a sense we do not disturb it at all, unless you remember that in order to see it we have to bounce light off it; and bouncing light off something gives it a tiny but definite impact, knocking it in a direction in which it would not have moved if we had not shone light on it. So although a billiard ball, being large enough, takes the impact of the light pretty well in its stride, when we try to observe an atom by shining light or X rays on it, we may in fact disturb it to an enormous extent, and this results in the famous Uncertainty Principle of Werner Heisenberg. I am not going to stay with that, but one remembers his principle: that there is a definite limit to the precision with which we can make predictions about atomic systems, simply because observing a system is deriving information not about the system alone, but about a relationship between the system and you. You observe *interactions.* You do not observe systems by themselves, but interactions between systems and your instruments; and hence statements made about the system by itself are definitely limited in their precision.

So much, then, for the problem of detachment. The second problem is that of defining a suitable language; and this, I think, is a little more interesting from my present standpoint. Right up to the end of the last century, scientists had always assumed that there must be one single language-system—one single connected set of ideas—in terms of which everything could be described if only we were clever enough. In the study of light, for example, there was considerable debate between people who thought that the right language to use about light was a language describing it in terms of wave motions, and those who thought that light should be pictured as a stream of particles—and oddly enough, there was a great deal of evidence supporting both standpoints. But at the turn of the century, evidence turned up which led people inevitably to conclude that it was not to be a matter of a *choice* between describing light as wave motion and describing it as particles, but that we had to have *both* languages. In this field, one language was not enough; you had to have two complementary languages.

This notion of *complementarity* was a new idea for physicists—and for almost everyone else. The idea that it was possible to say that light behaves like waves, which are continuous things, *and* that light behaves like a stream of discrete particles, sounded self-contradictory. And of course it would be a complete contradiction were it not that the situations in which light behaves like waves are different from those in which light behaves like particles. In fact, the language that you have to use is determined by the way in which you have decided to interact with the light. If you interact with the light by making it fall on a detecting instrument—by studying light on *impact*—then it turns out that you have to make your description in terms of particles. If you interact with the light by guiding it in *motion*, then it turns out that you have to use the language of waves, describing the light in terms of waves. The same holds for other entities such as cathode rays, which used to be thought of only as particles. The detailed technicalities are not at all important for our present purpose. I have mentioned them only to illustrate that in science we have discovered that different ways of interacting with a system may lead to quite different descriptions which are not contradictory but complementary, because the situation in which you need to use the one is different from the situation in which you need to use the other.

As a simple sort of analogy of this kind of relationship between two complementary descriptions, you might take the architect's practice of doing plan and elevation drawings of a building. On a plan drawing, you have details which you cannot see on the elevation, and on the elevation drawing you have details that you cannot see on the plan drawing, for the simple reason that each is drawn from a different standpoint. In order to comprehend the whole, you have to do a kind of mental synthesis of what it would look like from both standpoints at once. Somehow or other we are able to do this pretty well, even though in fact, if we looked at the real thing, we could see only one view or another according to our standpoint.

So to summarize this example from the field of physics: in studying atomic events we find first that total withdrawal is impossible, that in fact we have to be content with a definitely limited amount of predictability; and, second, that, because there are fundamentally two different methods of interacting with an atomic system, we must use two languages and not merely one to describe the system. We will come across similar points now in connection with our second and main subject of this chapter, the scientific study of man.

The Scientific Study of Man

In the case of the atom, one recalls, the trouble was that the system was so small that the least disturbance we could give to it in observing it knocked it appreciably off course. Man is a large animal, a good deal larger than a billiard ball, and certainly we do not expect the same kind of unpredictability to apply in the case of man as applies in the case of the atom. In fact, I would like to say in passing that I think that we ought to beware of stressing the implications of Heisenberg's Uncertainty Principle in the case of human beings; above all, I do not think it provides the true answer to the old problem of free will and determinism.

But the trouble with man as a scientific subject is that he is himself, of course, an observer: that the system being observed is itself an observer. The scientist studying man, like the philosopher of religion, then, is dealing with a sensitive system, in the sense of a system which *amplifies* the effects of his observations. However little you disturb a man by observing him, if the man knows that he is being observed this may have a large-scale effect, so that the man magnifies the effect of your disturbance on him. In engineering jargon, there is "feedback" in the situation.

A typical example of this, well known to industrial psychologists, arises in what is called time-and-motion study. People thought it would be a very good idea if psychologists could study men at work in a factory, observe how fast they moved, how long it took them to do certain things and so forth, so that in the interests of efficiency one could design the factory accordingly. It soon became known that this was going on; and of course in a very large number of cases the reliability of the results dropped sharply as soon as the men knew what was happening. A man naturally argues, "If I work at top speed today, then I shall be expected to work at top speed every day, so I had better go a little more slowly than I normally do." This is the kind of thing I mean. By observing human beings you may cause disturbances in them on a large scale, no matter how little you are interacting with them; and hence, any predictions that you would like to make as a scientist are liable to be invalidated as a result of this interaction.

There is a second difficulty in achieving withdrawal—the scientific prerequisite for prediction—in the study of human systems, namely, that if your prediction becomes known it can invalidate itself. This is, of course, the same logical point with which we started, that a predictor cannot predict the future of a system which includes itself. If, for example, you apply high-powered statistical methods to the Stock Exchange with a view to investing optimally, your prediction might perhaps be valid as long as you do not invest. But as soon as you allow your decisions to be influenced by your prediction, you are in danger of invalidating the basis on which you have made the prediction; and this is quite fundamentally inevitable, because no matter how you try to revise your prediction to allow for the effect of your influence on the system, as soon as you act upon the basis of the revised prediction, you begin invalidating the basis; it is an endless regression.

The same thing happens, of course, in social studies and political studies. It may be (in many systems it is so), that the *more* accurate your prediction, the more devastating will be its effect on the basis of prediction if you allow it to affect the system. So in any such situation, if your aim in making a prediction is to act upon the system on the basis of the prediction, there is a very severe limit on the reliability of your action. The kind of observer-predictor relationship with man-in-the-mass is not quite as politically powerful a relationship as it might seem. One might perhaps, with the help of science fiction, have thought at one time that the advent of high-speed computers could in principle enable our governors to predict all that we were going to do in such a way that our society would become a perfectly controlled machine with no free will of its own. Since, however, the only purpose of governors in predicting would be to act on the basis of their predictions, in doing so they would certainly restore to us the freedom to falsify their predictions in any respect in which our *physical* liberty was not restrained.

The Problem of Choice of Language

We shall find some of the most interesting limitations of the relationship of the observer-predictor in the study of man in the problem of choice of language.

It is a commonplace, of course, that my experience is best and most simply described, to me anyway, in subjective terms; but, of course, these are terms which the observer-predictor is precluded from using. By his terms of reference, he must use terms defined from a detached standpoint. He has, in fact, to deal with signs or symptoms of objective impressions, as observed from outside. In choosing a language from the observer's standpoint to describe a human being, there are many levels open to us. For instance, if I want to describe what happens as I meet a friend, I might say: "As I open the door, a mass of pink protoplasm rises to the height of five-and-a-half feet and begins to pucker and wobble up and down noisily"; or I might say, "He rises to his feet, smiles, and greets me warmly," or I might give all sorts of description in between. The biochemist could give one in one language, the psychologist in another, and the philosopher of religion in yet another. There are, then, different levels of language at which we can choose to make the observer description.

The work of a friend of mine happens to be concerned with trying to describe what goes on in the brain in physical terms, and to focus our ideas we might take a typical problem of the sort he is concerned with: suppose that I decide to move my finger, what is it that goes on at the same time in my head? For many years it was generally agreed, both among those who took the Hebraic view of the nature of man and those who did not, that if there were anything in the doctrine of the mind or the soul, one ought to come up against some evidence of it (when one tried to push the physical description far enough) in the form of a *gap* in the physical chain of cause and effect. In other words, both those who were in favor of the traditional Jewish conception of man and those who were against it in the name of so-called materialism, were agreed that evidence for the mind should be expected or sought in some kind of breakdown of physical method at some point in the physical description of the brain and nervous system.

So the need for another language, it was believed, could be shown by trying to push the one language to its limits; you would come across gaps, breakdowns, failures into which you had to bring something of the other language in order to close the gaps. For example, in the case of my decision to move my finger, the argument was, on the one side, that if you could trace the chain of cause and effect back into the brain you would find some sort of gap into which my decision came; and, on the other side, that if you did not find any gaps, then of course my decision was a "mere figment" and the "real thing" was the physical description, which was complete. I think this is a fallacy, and I believe it arises from a mistaken view of the relationship between the two languages in question: the physical language and, if you like, the mental language—the language in terms of decision, choice, responsibility, and so forth.

Complementary Descriptions of Human Activity

What I want to suggest and to work out a little is that these two languages are not rivals but, like the wave and particle descriptions of light (though not in the same way), they are complementary. I want to stress that they are not complementary in the way in which waves and particles or plan and elevation drawings are, because in these pairs of descriptions both are conceptually on the same level. There is not much difference between the conceptual level of a plan and an elevation drawing. The difference is one of standpoint only. I think a better idea of the relation of the two languages may be obtained by considering an electric advertising sign, made up of a large number of electric light bulbs on a board forming the outline of an advertisement—say, "Torah Does You Good." If you were to ask an electrician what was on the board, he could give a complete description of what was there in terms of light bulbs and wires—a description so complete that you could make a perfect replica of this sign anywhere in the world. Undoubtedly he has left nothing out; but he has not mentioned the "advertisement" or any of the words in it. On the other hand, it would be rather foolish to start an argument with him as to whether he had left something out, because the relationship of the one language to the other is one of complementarity; one is complementary to the other. You find the advertisement not through discovering a fault or a gap in the electrician's self-sufficient description, but by starting all over again with a different attitude to the same data, with a readiness to *read* the sign.

Roughly, the point I want to stress is that the terms in which a question is posed determine the language in which an answer can be sought. If we want to know why light bulb number 59 is out, then by asking the question in those terms we invite an answer in electrical language. Conversely, if somebody is ill-advised enough to put up an erroneous statement in electric lights, it is no good accusing the electrician of incompetence. It is not an electrical defect. The question, What is right or wrong with this advertisement? is not answered in electrical terms.

These are, of course, trivial illustrations; but they bring out the first point, which I think will bear a lot of further exploration: the terms or the language in which you frame your question define for you the terms or the language in which you should properly expect an answer. The reason is simply that any answer which you could attempt to give in the wrong language would already be the answer to a different question, a question phrased in that language. Suppose, for example, we came across the answer "Because the wire is cut to light bulb 59." This is an answer to the question of the form "Why doesn't bulb 59 light?" You cannot use it alone as an answer to a question of the form "Why is this advertisement true or false?" Still, one reason why the advertisement offers a better analogy than the others is that there are some ways in which, in practice, we often do sum up both descriptions in one sentence. For instance, we might say, "I am going to switch on the advertisement," when we mean we are going to switch on the electric current to the light bulbs. In just the same way, when we speak about man we very often do not mean only one description or the other; we very often mean both, in a rather loose way.

This brings me to a second point: in order that any statement about the system be true in the one language, it is necessary for some statement to be true in the other. In order that I should say anything at all in advertising language about what is on the board (assuming that I can see it only when it is lit), it is necessary for some electrical statement to be true about what is on the board. Something must be true about the path of electric currents, in order that something describing words delineated on the board may be true. And yet this necessity is not, I think, properly described as a relationship of *causality*. This is perhaps the point I want to emphasize most: that you can have relationships of *necessity* which are not relationships of *causality* in the ordinarily accepted sense of the word. To take an example, where the term "cause" comes in more naturally: if I write $2x + 3 = 5$ on the blackboard, then in order that any statement, true or false, be on the board, it is necessary that there be chalk on the board and that some description in terms of chalk particles be true. But $2x + 3$ is not equal to 5 *because* the chalk particles are in position. It is a relationship of necessity, of complementarity, but not of causality; it is nonsense to speak of one fact as the "cause" of the other.

Now this has direct bearing on the typical question with which this chapter began. When I decide to move my finger, how is my decision related to what goes on in my brain? Very briefly, I suggest that terms such as decision, choice, and so on are words defined from my standpoint as agent or "actor" in the situation; they form a language of their own, and if I ask what was the cause of my decision to move my finger, the primary answer must be in the same language. It is not good trying to say that the cause of my decision was electro-chemical events in my brain. The reason is that any answer in terms of electro-chemical events in my brain is already the answer to a different question, namely, "What was the cause of the physical movement observed?" You can put it this way: physiology enables us, in principle, to trace the pattern of cause and effect right back from the finger movement to the electrical impulses in nerve fibers, to somewhere else where it gets lost in the scurry of activity inside the head. No one has begun to trace out the full pattern here, but there has been no evidence so far that normal physical entailment fails. Consequently, we could translate our original question by asking, "What is the relationship between my decision and the physical events in my head which give rise to the movement of my finger—the physical correlate of my decision?" It is here, I suggest, that the relationship is one of necessity and complementarity, but not causality. In other words, my decision is related to the physio-chemical events in my brain not as cause and effect, but in the kind of way that the description in advertising language is related to the description in electrical language. The one is necessary in order that the other should come about, but it is linguistic nonsense to try to say that one is the cause of the other in the sense in which one would say that the pressing of a button is the cause of the ringing of an electrical bell.

There is not space here to discuss the bearing of this on the ancient problem of free will and determinism, beyond suggesting that if we take the typical questions which have been posed in relation to free will and physical determinism and sift them for language systems asking to what language system each term belongs, I think we shall find a good many instances of mixing of terms from different language systems in the posing of these traditional questions.

Now I do not suppose that many of us have ever felt very seriously that a complete physical description of man would "debunk" Judaism. But there are, I suppose, those who do; and I hope it may be clear from this discussion where the fallacy in such debunking lies. Debunking or, as I like to call it, "nothing buttery" (the doctrine that man is "nothing but" a pattern of chemicals, etc.) arises, I think, from the logical fallacy of confusing *exclusiveness* with *exhaustiveness.* To come back to the illustration of the advertising sign, the electrician's account may properly be described as exhaustive. It has left nothing out;

there is nothing left if he takes away everything on the board according to his description. But, it is not in any sense *exclusive*. Your description of what is on the board in the words of the advertisement is just as valid at the end of his exhaustive description as it was before, and you do not improve his description by adding at the end of it, "Oh, and there's also an advertisement saying 'Torah Does You Good.'" It does not belong there.

And so, equally, I think, the physicist has grounds for hoping that in principle (not in practice, because you disturb the system far too much) a physical description of the processes of the brain could be complete—exhaustive—in the sense that there would be no gaps into which you would have to fit nonphysical processes. But although exhaustive in this sense, it would be in no way exclusive of the description which we would normally give in subjective terms of our own decisions, choices, and responsibilities.

Perhaps I might add one final remark. As a Jew, I have found this case of the scientific study of man, and the relationship between the physical description of man and the mental description, a most helpful and stimulating parable of the age-old mystery of the relationship between the activity of God and the physical events which the scientist studies. I do not mean to suggest in any sense the pantheistic conclusion that God is just the world we know viewed from a different standpoint, an issue I have treated in an earlier chapter dealing with Spinoza's ethics; but it seems to me that if one does take the various hints which Torah offers as to the relationship of God with the world, it bears much more this stamp of complementarity than of any simple pushbutton causality. To take just one example, the Psalmist speaks of God "sending his rain upon the mountains" and so on; and he speaks in these terms about so many events for which even he must have known an alternative account in more physical terms that we would obviously be missing the point if we took his words as an alternative (rival) explanation of the physical cause of the rain. He is using a language complementary with whatever scientific description we can give; and in fact I think that the relationship between most of the religious descriptions of God's activity and what a scientist might have said had he been present are at least permissively of this logical sort. That is to say, I think it may be worthwhile exploring the *possibility* that in each case the "activity of God" is related to the activity observed by human beings, not causally but complementarily in this sense.

May I summarize two key points which I have endeavored to make clear in this section. First, that scientific observation alone cannot give any man the power over his fellows which he has over a machine, as long as he wishes to exercise that power, which is, of course, what we mean by having power; and that in fact the withdrawal necessary for the complete prediction of a system precludes you from interacting with it and using the knowledge that you gain. Second, that in any one rational or "objective" description of Judaism, as of other systems, we commit ourselves to a choice of standpoint and of abstractive level which is only one among many, and that the validity of descriptions in different language systems must be judged within each language system itself and cannot safely be judged by reference to any description to another language system. This does not mean that the two are totally independent (something must be true in the one language in order that something may be true in the other, and we have come across relationships of necessity between statements in the one language and statements in the other); but the proper criteria of their truth and falsehood are expressed, and can only be applied, in terms of their own language systems. In particular, the validity of any questions of decision, choice, and responsibility can be judged, and these questions can be properly answered, only in the language systems of decision, choice, and responsibility.

7

Meaningful Relativism

The social and cultural advance of religious man is, as I have already stated, directly related to the development of personality. This has been, and still is, a very slow and gradual affair. Even now man has achieved only a limited awareness of himself as personality. At the very threshold of history, our primitive ancestors lived in what Lucien Lévy-Bruhl has well described as a *participation mystique,* a mystical sharing with nature. At this stage, there was still no clear differentation in man's mind between himself and his environment. Only later, as man grew slowly toward an awareness of himself as personality, did it become possible for him to see both himself and the external world in relation to one another, and so to transcend his earlier containment within the dark forces of nature.

This growth of a sense of relatedness brought with it something else, the first stirrings of the scientific consciousness. For man, now beginning to become aware of himself, could begin to see nature as something "other," as phenomena standing apart, which could be observed and investigated. But the differentation of man from nature was, if I may so express it, only the permissive condition for the growth of true science. Something else was needed.

It is clear to me that modern science could not have come into being until the ancient pagan conception of the natural world had given place to the Hebraic. The pagan world-view was largely atomistic. Each separate event was ruled by its own constellation of conditioning impulses. With the monotheism of the Bible came something new: the assertion of a creation by a God who was not only Creator but also Lawgiver to his creation. This belief predisposed man's mind to an enhanced empathy with the unitary character of the universe, grounded in the faith that man is made in the image of the One God. Another step was taken with the development of eschatological thought in postexilic Judaism—the mysteries of messianism, and much later, Zionism's confident hope that in the fullness of time he would gather together all Jews in a restored and renewed Zion.

As time went on, however, the phenomenal achievements of science fostered a sense of human power and self-sufficiency that was antithetical to traditional exilic humility. Practical success was a heady and intoxicating draught. For Laplace in the eighteenth century, God had become a hypothesis which science no longer needed. Why indeed could not man himself become as God? Was he not the master in a mechanistic universe that human science could both explain and control?

The further development of science, not to speak of other phenomenal causes, has itself exposed the hollowness of these pretensions. In the new climate of scientific thought, old certainties have become uncertain, eternal truths have lost their timelessness. Perhaps the most important factor responsible for this change has been the virtual replacement of the observer-predictor attitude by the activity of the observer-participant. The ideal of eliminating the scientist's person from the process of experiment, so as to achieve the highest degree of objectivity, has had to be abandoned in one field after another. Indeed, the gap between the observer and the observed field or system cannot any longer be kept open, for man himself is involved. This subject will be treated at greater length in the following chapter.

As long as he could persuade himself that he was looking at facts "objectively," man could feel secure. Now the indubitable "fact" has again become a mystery. Pure objectivity is now seen to be pure illusion. The recognition of the observer's own involvement in what he is observing has again restored man's psyche to its central position in the scheme of things, to a position from which the scientists of earlier centuries hoped they had removed it forever.

Since man is potentially a unity and a totality in himself, he is inescapably committed to the search for unity in the world of experience. This inner potentiality in man, which ever seeks to realize itself as a unity, is what I propose to call personality. The word "personality" is so important that I must try to define it as precisely as possible. But it is very difficult to circumscribe by definition, for personality is not a "thing" but a living and developing system. We may describe it as an organic unity, an intimate fusion of what man is with everything he does. But man's actions depend not only upon the conscious mind; they are conditioned to a high degree by the unconscious. His personality—the organic complex of thoughts, desires, impulses, actions, and memories which make him what he is—embraces both conscious and unconscious elements in perpetually changing interplay. As long as man is unaware of this close interrelation, he is only partially aware of himself as a personality. I believe, therefore, that the ground and aim of our human existence may be summed up as the achievement of a relationship of awareness to personality.

Such awareness is the precondition of our being able to function, either as a contributing and responding part of a greater whole or as a personality in our own right. It is the integration of the unconscious with the conscious which in the end leads to awareness of true personality, awareness of the self.

This self cannot exist in isolation; it is only "there," as it were, as the nodal point of a system of interrelations to which every aspect of life's many-sided richness makes its contribution. The difficulty of conveying the true sense of this concept is obvious, for the center of personality is not something that can be observed and measured in the same way that we observe and measure the behavior of matter. And yet we are all to some degree aware of its meaning. Today people are beginning slowly to realize that there has been a shift from the center, that modern Judaism, together with modern man, has become "off center." Through identification with particular aspects of life at the expense of others, we have produced abstracts of man in many varieties. These go by such names as "scientific man," "economic man," "secular man," "political man," and the like. In all this there is a great danger, because a shifting away from the center makes man less than himself; the false selves he creates cannot satisfy him. This is why in our present society there is so widespread a sense of meaninglessness about our existence. We have forgotten that our grandest challenge lies in the development of ourselves as full personalities. Instead we degrade personality to a means serving an end, and forget that personality is an end and purpose in itself. Man today suffers within his own soul the tyrannical rule of the part over the whole. The shifting of the self, as the vital center of personality, out to the periphery, and its identification with narrow specialisms, has led directly to the impersonality of modern life, has distorted personal relationships and falsified our recognition of personal and collective responsibility.

But how can man be helped to achieve a sound relationship to himself and fulfill his eternal task of growth from potential to actual personality? In ancient times, over the porch of the Delphic oracle were written the words "Know Thyself." Present-day psychology also attempts to approach the uncertainties of human existence through self-knowledge. Freud revived this ancient wisdom by looking at man mainly in his family relationships. For him the whole process of the development of the psyche depended ultimately upon the integration of the child-parent relation. In Freud's view all cultural progress, as well as the achievement of moral order, rested upon this integration. Jung widened the psychological horizon to take in the whole interrelated range of human experience. Nevertheless, at the center of both the Freudian and Jungian approaches to the psyche lies the notion of the growth and development of personal awareness of two primary modes of human reaction: first, of the role of the instincts, and second, of that of the archetypes. For this discussion, I propose to confine myself to the archetypes.

Though the word "archetype" may still sound strange to many ears, it has an honorable history. Long before it became a fundamental concept in analytical psychology, it was used by the Bible. In the book of Genesis we learn that man does not come into being or perish of his own volition or by the exigencies and whims of an indifferent nature that prescribes "necessity," but rather, that everything which does come into being and perishes is said to be formed according to God's will. This primary will of God is not only the source of all things, because God is eternal and because he remains the same and unchangeable. Through participation in God's will, it happens that everything is what it is and how it is.

Etymologically, the word "archetype" is derived from the Greek words *arche,* first, foremost or chief; and *tupos,* a blow or the mark left by a blow, an impress or a mold. We are familiar with the first element in such words as "archipelago," "architect," "archbishop"; and with the second in "type," "typical," and so on. The word "archetype" as used in analytical psychology is perhaps best rendered as "master pattern." The archetypes are held to belong to man's remotest inheritance. They are patterns of behavior through which his actions are unconsciously conditioned, and may therefore be regarded as a priori categories reaching back into levels of experience where man neither knows nor remembers.

It is difficult to explain the idea of the archetype in logical propositions, for its meaning can be fully grasped only through personal experience. I will, however, try to bring as much illumination to the question as I can by considering how the archetypes actually operate, first in imaginative artistic creation, and second in the activity of communication.

Let us then look first at the archetypes as a priori categories of the imagination. May I elucidate the meaning of this somewhat enigmatic formulation with a brief discussion of what may be termed "moments of vision," which in painting and poetry alike emerge with unpredictable vividness to dominate a whole work of art. It may be suggested that the clue to the compulsive, all-embracing character of these experiences may well be the feeling of self-discovery or self-identification that often accompanies them. In other words, the "moment of vision" is related "to something within us that already and forever exists." This last phrase is from an essay by Coleridge. Here is the whole passage from which it is taken:

> In looking at objects . . . as at yonder moon dim glimmering through the dewy pane, I seem rather to be seeking, as it were asking a

> symbolical language for something within me that forever and already exists, than observing anything new. Even when that latter is the case yet still I have always an obscure feeling, as if that new phenomenon were a dim awakening of a forgotten or hidden truth of my inner nature.

In somewhat different terms, a sense of reality is a conquest, an advance from the chaos and confusion of an unintelligible world: a construction. The first order introduced into man's conception of the world was an aesthetic order—the order of ritual and myth. Later the intellect gradually made a selection of the totality—the part it can describe and measure—and gave it a more or less coherent unity, and called it science. The map is constantly enlarged: new details are filled in; but vast territories of space and time must still be marked "terra incognita." The religious *qua* aesthetic sensibility plays like lightning over these dark abysses, and in the flashes gets a brief glimpse of the lineaments of this unknown: the brief glimpse that is the artist's intuition, and which he then strives to communicate to us by the symbols he invents. That is the moment of originality—the moment in which we are made to realize the ethereal, shimmering texture of music, the shapes that haunt thought's wilderness in poetry, the "beauty wrought out from within upon the flesh" of a painting. Poetry, painting, music—all these are arts of skills for raising the senses to that condition of insight in which the world is not transfigured but in which for the first time some aspect of it is revealed, or made real, and thereby, for human eyes, newly created, newly communicated.

And now a few words on the archetypes as modes of communication. Both religion and science are essentially concerned with the communication of experience through symbols. It may even be argued that the essential act of thought is symbolization. After all, it is the same with thought as it is with spoken or written language, where every combination of sounds and letters stands for (or symbolizes) the experience that lies behind its meaning. Man, or more precisely the human psyche, is the channel through which deepest experience finds expression and communicates its essential quality. In other words, we may say that man is the medium through which life becomes conscious of itself.

Artistic creation is one of the highest expressions of communication. But in the creative work of the great artist, whether conveyed in words, music, color, or form, we recognize, no matter how infinitely varied the specific imagery may be, a universal character. The explanation lies in the universality of the archetypal content which infuses and gives form to the experience which the artist re-creates and communicates. Although the particular symbolism employed will vary from one culture to another, and from one artist to another, the symbols necessarily illustrate a theme. The fact that they constitute "variations on a theme" does not justify us in refusing to recognize that the theme itself is in the highest degree meaningful. We may sum this up by quoting C. G. Jung's unambiguous statement that "the archetype is not the consequence of physical facts, but rather shows how physical facts are experienced by the soul."

What holds true for art holds true also for communication between persons. We can experience in a relation with another person a kind of communication, almost of communion, which goes far beyond what is mediated by the physical senses alone. In such a relation, we in fact comprehend the "thou" in symbols. The validation of these symbols must vary to some degree in accordance with the psychological situation in which the persons concerned are involved. But the mode of communication is essentially governed by the same archetypal patterns that are at work in artistic communication. Transference phenomena in psycho-analytical practice are also manifestations of archetypal communication. They are synchronous experience between two psychic systems.

From what has been said up till now, it is clear that the archetypes are collective in the sense that they are common to all men. Analytical psychology asserts that the propensity to use archetypal modes is innate in human beings. It believes that the archetypes are inherited in much the same way as the instincts. Man's image-forming proclivity is a manifestation of his archetypal heritage. It is the power of imaging that is inherited, and not necessarily the symbols employed, though the widespread use and acceptance of particular symbols shows that they too are generally recognized as adequate expressions of archetypal experiences.

Before I turn in the next chapter to the matter of scientific, vis-à-vis religious, communication, another and vitally important question must now be considered, that of archetypal motivation in social and political thought and institutions. For it is very necessary for us to understand how archetypal motifs may inform political thinking and find expression in social institutions. Institutions, after all, are made by men; and much may depend on our awareness of the psychological soil in which they are rooted. Take, for example, political power and its institutional organization. Political authority is necessarily and of its very nature social. It operates in a multilateral system of mutual relationships which distributes appropriate roles to all the members of society, from the least to the most powerful. What happens if we replace "social" by "personal"? The answer is Hitler's Germany or Stalin's Russia. The clue is already given by these phrases, which equate a country with a person. The effect is that the emotions bound up with archetypal authority are now focused on an individual, who thereby—since the archetype is indestructible—is placed beyond removal and even beyond criticism; his word is the law. Where the archetypal background of political authority is seen, not as social, but in a personalized way, love and justice are the first casualties.

This is what happens under personal dictatorships. But there are totalitarian systems without personal dictators: What is it that makes them so widely acceptable today? We can discern one important reason in the depersonalized character of almost all modern societies: that is, their tendency (mentioned earlier) to press the individual into a specialized mold, so that he lives as a "part-man" and is cut off from a full experience of personality. Under these conditions man's need to transform himself through unitary experience may well be projected onto the symbols of a totalitarian political system. Putting this another way, we may say that the psychological drive behind contemporary totalitarianism is man's unconscious, but frustrated, desire to experience himself as a full person. What happens in the political climate of totalitarianism is that the self, or rather a caricatured form of it, is projected onto a powerful person. This human symbol, the "leader" or "dictator," has power over us by virtue of the fact that we have projected our selves upon him. All this can happen only when we ourselves are "off-center."

It is of crucial importance to realize that the impulse to project the individual self onto a social symbol is inspired by unconscious archetypal forces, which for the want of a better term must be called religious. Only if free societies achieve awareness and understanding of this fact will they be able to find the answer of political totalitarianism whether of the Right or the Left. The citizen of a totalitarian society does not distinguish his own individuality from the collective symbol, and so allows the state to become in the end the only arbiter of moral values. The Leviathan, the all-demanding state, is incompatible with the fulfillment of personality. As long as man is regarded as merely a product of society, he is thereby reduced to the level of the primitive. He cannot cooperate with his environment because he is contained within it. In this respect, his thinking is prelogical. His undifferentiated consciousness, his lack of relationship to personality, reflects his lack of relationship to the organs of government of his society. He is submerged in his political system by reason of the projection of his unitary self onto his society. The symbolism of the totalitarian state derives its compelling power from the fact that it represents an exteriorization of the archetype self in a distorted form.

The evolution of consciousness and the growing awareness of the self's relationship to the archetypes are closely bound up with man's search for freedom. This is inevitable for us because freedom is the ultimate ethical expression of Judaism's deep-seated urge to grow toward full personality. Individual freedom, psychologically understood, is a function of the fully matured personality. This is not to say that a Jew, by becoming consciously aware of them, can cut himself off from his archetypal ancestral roots. They will still be there whether he is conscious of them or not. But there is all the difference in the world between the Jew who is aware of his problem, and the Jew who is unconsciously ruled by it. The former is, to the extent of his awareness, free; the latter is inevitably bound.

I have left to the end one of the most difficult questions of all. It is whether there is any certain evidence for the existence of the archetypes; and if so, what sort of evidence it may be. In one sense, we can certainly speak of proof; in another sense, we can say that it is quite impossible to produce objective proof of the existence of the archetypes. In the physical sciences, we use concepts such as "atom" and "electron" for entities that are not directly observable. There can therefore be no "proof" of their existence. But the evidence for their existence derives from observation—the observation of phenomena which they serve to explain. To ask "what" they are is meaningless; for the only way to answer this question would be to describe them in terms of something directly observable and familiar. In fact, they are equated with energy, and energy, as Bertrand Russell puts it, "is not defined except as regards its laws and the relation of changes in its distribution to our sense." In other words, we know of something we call energy by inference from observed phenomena; for the same reason, we postulate the existence of those complexes of energy which we call atoms and electrons.

Similarly, it is no use asking "what" the archetypes "are"; we infer the existence of these "master patterns" because they are the best way of explaining certain psychic phenomena—the potent, emotionally charged symbolic images which figure in dreams and also in waking mental life. Because we find closely similar images occurring in the dreams and imaginings of many different individuals, often apparently without being related to any experience in the individual's life, we infer that they derive from a heritage of experience, going far back into history, which has no doubt been common to some large part of mankind, but perhaps almost excruciatingly clear to Jews throughout history. The empirical interpretation of this common stock of symbolical representations lights up and makes understandable to us our own psychological attitudes and behavior, and in addition provides us with a criterion of judgment.

All this may seem far removed from the quantitative thinking and experimental methods characteristic of the physical sciences. But should we allow this to worry us unduly? It is true enough that the methodology of the physical sciences is largely inapplicable to the fields either of individual or of social psychology (though even this assertion should not be pushed too far). On the other hand, while the experimental techniques appropriate to the investigation of physical nature have, through their successful application in their own field, come to color our thinking to a great degree, we should not allow ourselves, because of this, to forget or underestimate the validity of image thinking. With the verbal expression of ideas, we are all familiar. With the equally valid use of symbols, much less so.

Image thinking is archetypal cognition. It is a mode of experiencing reality in which the mind comprehends as a whole. The revelatory character of a scientific discovery as distinct from its detailed validation is experienced as a flash of illumination. It is a moment of originality and awe. Doubtless, if the process were analyzed, we should find that the whole mental apparatus of memory, sensation, and the rest was involved. Nevertheless, it remains a total response of the personality in which the unitary character of the scientist's mind creatively comprehends a single process. Science advances by bringing ever-wider aggregations of data under ever-simpler categories. In this process we may see the archetype of unity at work. Since man is potentially a unity and totality in himself, he is inescapably committed to the attempt to experience the world as unity.

We can see the same power at work in the discovery of mental phenomena. In a moment of heightened awareness, the discovery of mental interrelations, unrealized before, has a unique and compelling quality which derives from the fact that the whole of our potentialities of perception is engaged. The whole is more than the sum of its parts; it is that "plus" which accounts for the compelling, numinous quality which we find in archetypal experience. The unitary character of archetypal apperception conveys in the fullest sense a feeling of truth. It is "knowing" in the deepest sense; and precisely because it is not and cannot be "willed," it is an experience of true creativity. In this way validation turns into verification; a proof for the experiencing individual as solid as any scientific proof could possibly be. When an individual is brought to find meaning in an otherwise meaningless existence, this is for him "proof" of the validity of archetypal experience.

8

A Phenomenology of Religious Communication

To speak in somewhat more detailed terms of the phenomenological and linguistic challenges and dilemmas of one specific form of religious communication, namely prayer, even if we make every allowance for the exaggerations of the genetic method—which professes to find the key of existing ideas and beliefs in the knowledge of their origins, so that, to fix a religion's origin is equivalent to saving or condemning it—it cannot be denied that the knowledge of that astounding moment in which the soul awakes to prayer is of incalculable interest and importance.

In order to acquire this knowledge, two methods have traditionally been attempted. One has sought the origin of prayer on the "outside," so to speak, whether in a historic revelation or in a product (idiogenetic or heterogenetic) of social life. Another has tried to find it within the interior world of man, whether in beliefs or in particular emotions.

Here a question of general character is involved, a question which has troubled many modern Jewish thinkers particularly, ever since they attempted to decide whether in Judaism one ought to give precedence to intellectual or to emotional values. For them, this question involved the philosophic differences of the intellectuals and the voluntarists, who labored hard in contrary directions to determine which of the two psychical activities—intellect or will—ought to have preference over the other.

Where this philosophic struggle was transferred wholly to the field of investigation of the "facts" of Jewish faith, the point that had to be settled was whether precedence would be granted to myth or to ritual. But owing to their absorption in the detailed examination of religious "facts," secular Jewish historians have often failed to bear in mind that Judaism could never become merely a single function of the intellect, as may be the case with philosophical inquiry, nor could it ever be confined to a system of rituals or of "rules" of life. Even in primitive religions—where sometimes it had been possible to see the myth reduced to the position of a rational gloss or comment on the particular rite—the same principle holds good.

This rational comment finds its analogy in a more advanced religion when, through a fresh (and periodic) systematization of knowledge, philosophy of religion is often reduced to the level of finding reasons for primitive dogmas and cultic beliefs which had either lost their original meaning through the passage of time or had retained a partitive meaning which could no longer be accepted as "reasonable." Here came into play the natural tendency to make "intelligible" and "moral," as far as possible, the irrational elements of religion.

But in reality, if myth is to have a religious significance (though it is not necessary that it always should), if it is not to be a mere exercise of creative fancy or imagination, as often happens in various antique religions of animism, it does not arise without a corresponding emotion, which, like the myth to which it refers, becomes an element in religion and a *terminus a quo* for a cult.

Similarly, one may say that a cult could not maintain its position unless it presupposed a myth or a body of beliefs. History, in fact, offers no example of a religion which does not possess myths, beliefs, cults, and rites—though it may perhaps in a quite rudimentary form. And the reason for this is because these are not separable one from the other, as are the rules of life which are drawn from them. To maintain, therefore, as has sometimes been done, that religion can dispense with one or the other, shows a misconception of its nature and of its function in human life.

Equally unreliable is the old hypothesis which has maintained that cults, like religions, have grown up in the interest of the state organization through the action of astute politicians or grasping priests, who were determined to cultivate in the people the fear of divine chastisement. As this hypothesis arose from actual experience of what religion is apt to become in the hands of "statesmen," one need not be surprised that it has found more than one supporter. Machiavelli knew quite well what authority religion gave to the prince when he said that ecclesiastical princedoms are obtained either by good conduct or by good fortune, and that they can be kept without either because they are upheld and validated by religious institutions.

Certainly this fact has lent support to the contention that governments, which are so interested in maintaining religions, are also the creators of it; and this has been the opinion of famous thinkers such as Thomas Hobbes and Voltaire. It has also had an influence in bringing about in other cases a fierce hostility toward established religions, the most notable of which in modern times is the thought of Karl Marx, who considered established religion to be an opiate for the people.

Hypotheses that have been more favored by recent ethnological and psychological researches are those which look for the origins of religion in the inner working of the soul or, to put it more concretely, in a discrete body of internal beliefs or in particular emotions. Intellectual preoccupations, such as that of studying the causes of phenomena; animistic or manistic beliefs; beliefs in mysterious impersonal forces, such as mana or orenda; beliefs in great beings or hero redeemers or founders of civilizations; or even curiosity, wonder, fear, the sense of absolute dependence; beliefs and feelings of a social character, such as fetishism and magic—such are said to be some of the original motives that, either together or separately, have given rise to religion and consequently to worship, under its three aspects of sacrifice, mystery, and prayer.

It is said, for example, that prayer has arisen from the relation of the man who prays to an ideal humanity; and this hypothesis has endeavored to find support by pointing to the general tendency to idealize man and the pains that people take in every stage of civilization to deck themselves in geegaws and ornaments rather than to dress in simple clothing. Euhemerus, who long ago held that the gods were nothing but glorified heroes, may be considered as a forerunner of the modern manistic hypothesis, which seeks to derive the origin of prayer from the worship of ancestors or savior heroes or founders of civilization—a worship which is still as widely spread and as ingrained in popular beliefs as it was with the ancient Egyptians, the Chinese, the Indians, the Greeks, and the Romans.

If we get down to the psychological basis of this anthropomorphic belief, we find that it has a solid foundation in an indestructible tendency of the human spirit and that, in spite of the condemnation of Immanuel Kant, it continues to flourish as much as ever. It seems in fact, according to certain aspects of the history of religion, that if man can ascribe to the Divine nothing but his own virtues idealized, he has been unable to find anything more worthy of adoration than himself. This is what led Ludwig Feuerbach in the nineteenth century to conclude that the origin of the idea of God is traceable to a projection of an idealized man and the idea of worship to an adoration of himself, or (if we express it in general terms as Auguste Comte does) an idealized humanity, the expression varying according to the degree of stress laid upon the personal or the social elements in religion.

Animism, which cannot any more than anthropomorphism be regarded as a religion in itself, is unable to afford any plausible explanation of the origin of worship. In fact, in order to explain the origin of either moral ideas or worship, animism has to resort to the superstructures of a subsequent development, which presents as suitable for worship objects to which the conscience can react in a specifically religious manner. It must, however, be admitted that when anthropomorphism and animism turn to the fostering of religion they bring out some of the fundamental aspects of prayer much better than the magic that preceded animism does.

For while it may be true that magic produces attitudes of mind similar to the attitudes of petition and propitiation so frequently found in prayer, yet the overmastering desire for domination and supremacy leads to an attitude very different from that of the man at prayer, who never exercises violence or coercion as does the magician. And just as for the purpose of prayer this impersonal force proves empty and lifeless, so animism and anthropomorphism prove pale and insignificant until the objects which they put forward for adoration have their skeletons clothed in a covering such as every object of worship requires.

Now without pursuing further these hypotheses on the origin of prayer, I hope that it will not be difficult from what I have said to realize that they fail to reveal a motive which would be sufficiently convincing and sufficiently abiding to account not only for the origin but also for the continuance of prayer down to our day.

This fact might have sufficed to raise in the minds of the upholders of these hypotheses a doubt as to whether they were on the right track. I must, however, before proceeding further, point out that the principal hypotheses on the origin of prayer take for granted as a matter of course something innate and fundamental in the human spirit in which the roots of prayer are sunk and out of which these hypotheses must in their turn consciously grow.

This is the case, for example, with the hypothesis—the most widely accepted one in Judaism—of a historical revelation, which has to assume a particular disposition of mind in order that it may be recognized as divine and may be faithfully accepted. Spinoza used to say that the prophets of Israel could not have known whether Yahweh had revealed himself to them if they had not somehow had in themselves an idea of the Divine; and Schelling added later that religion could not have come into existence had there not been a religious conscience in man.

The same may be said of the supposed discovery of the origin of prayer in the astuteness and cupidity of rulers and priests. This hypothesis not only fails to account for spontaneous prayer like the preceding one, but also fails to realize that the man who prays, whether through fear of divine punishment or to praise or give thanks, must, if he acts religiously, feel in some way the characteristic and unmistakable sense of the Divine. At any rate, he must react in some way to the divine which he has discovered in the object of his worship. On the other hand, neither the state nor the synagogue could make appeal to a final sanction of the ordinance or to the proved results of prayer unless they assumed the existence of some higher power, unless in other words, they derived their sanctions from some source beyond themselves.

Another question of a general nature about the origin of prayer has reference to its individual or social, its conscious or subconscious, coefficient. Psychologists lay emphasis now on the social and on the individual sources of prayer. Orthodox Christians usually prefer the former, Protestants the latter. But for Judaism, when people pray it is always through their own personal action, and if this action corresponds to an inner need (without which it is not true Judaism) it cannot be called a mere product of collectivity.

From estimating the individual and the social coefficient of the origin of prayer, men have been led to examine the part which reflex action plays in it. William James called this the greatest discovery of modern psychology, and from his time onward the irrational tendency of the soul to enter into relation with the invisible has been considered by several psychologists as an irradiation of subconscious action. They were thus enabled without difficulty to give an explanation of all the psychological characteristics of prayer. Freud and the psychoanalytical school have gone still further and have claimed that consciousness of guilt was suggested to humanity by the Oedipus complex and prayer by the libido. For the psychoanalysts, the mystical ecstasy and the sexual ecstasy are regarded as phenomena derived from the same source, and the need for prayer, reduced to its organic origins, is regarded as nothing more than a consequence of physiological distress, neurosis, and the sexual impulse. One is perfectly right in refusing to accept the identification of the normal and higher forms of prayer with those of psychopathic personalities. Still, one cannot altogether refuse to recognize the subconscious source of the desire for prayer, a source which, after all, is the great reservoir for biological tendencies, for aspirations, for impulses, for social and traditional inspirations.

Even the need of the human spirit for coming into contact with the one Supreme Being—a need that is at the foundation of any theocentric system which explains the origin of prayer—

must still be connected with the same subliminal source. As against the rationalists, the question has been raised whether their own dogma may not be a product of that obscure subliminal source; while as against the views of the individualists, Emile Durkheim explained the dogma as an impulse from collective energies that have found their way into the intelligence and the will.

The question may be put in the following terms: if the mystic life is represented as withdrawn from the intelligent and volitional action of the individual, is not this equivalent to seeing in it nothing but ephemeral manifestations and ignoring the laws of its normal development? If that is so, psychology will do well to find a midpoint between these two extremes, emphasizing the active personal, conscious aspect of prayer in contrast with those who see in it either a mere attitude of mind produced by specific ideas or by a simple uprush of the subconscious, an abandonment, an annihilation of the personality, a passive liberation of the innermost self, where all beings meet and love.

In the sources of Jewish prayer, it must be admitted, there are rational and irrational elements. Without the former, it would not make itself perceptible as a deep need of the spirit—a need which justifies itself by its mere appearance. Without the latter, it would not be possible to explain the specific character which prayer assumes in dependence on the system of revelation that inspires it. Among the irrational elements so conspicuous in Jewish prayer are the emotions of awe and joy. Some, however, have confused awe with that terrifying fear which ought to be left out of account as a direct source of religion and prayer; it excludes love, and therefore prayer which is inspired only by fear will never be religious. Awe, on the other hand, is associated with veneration and with love.

The religious source of prayer in Judaism cannot, therefore, be confused with the fear of punishment, nor can it be attributed in its relations to an idealized humanity or to associations suggested by fetishes or other natural objects (worship of animals, plants, stones, water, and fire) or by the need for assistance or defense on the part of living kinsmen. For the piety, the fear, the awe, the deep respect, and the other emotions that these relationships require are in no way the same as the religious relationship. Even the Christian theologian Friedrich Schleiermacher, although he did not perceive that his definition of religion took account only of a relationship and not of the two related terms, had at least recognized that the feeling of dependence could not, by itself, constitute the essence of religion; and, in order to distinguish it from every other feeling of dependence, he added that this feeling was absolute, or in other words, absolutely different from that feeling of dependence that may be experienced in relationships which are not religious.

In a similar way, the Romans distinguished between *sacra privata* and *sacra publica,* the honors rendered to the dead requiring different thought and feelings from those rendered to the gods. These hypotheses, however, did not make the necessary distinction between emotions that were religious and emotions that were not religious. They did not see that, however great the resemblances may appear, the two things fall under different categories. In one case, one of the related terms, even though idealized, is still always conceived of as human and profane; in the other case; it is clearly and definitely understood to be sacred. In the one, the impressive and mysterious movement of the stars, the majestic cycles of the seasons, of fair and foul weather, of the growth and decay of plants and of man is only an expression of the caprice of the spirits that direct them; while in the other, we are dealing with the Divine which lies hidden, like something entirely distinct, behind the phenomena of nature.

In fact, these hypotheses did not discover the line which makes a clear demarcation between the act that is religious and the act that is not; and therefore, they were not able to find the essential meaning of prayer. In partial justification of their attitude, it may be allowed that, at first view, prayer may appear to differ only quantitatively from the relationship between one human being and another, perhaps because of the persistent anthropomorphism which is constantly threatening to turn the Divine into the human. That it does, however, differ qualitatively as well may be seen from a brief consideration of the two terms which form this relationship: the Divine and the religious emotion which responds to it. Prayer must be a translation into action of this relationship.

I am indebted to a number of modern mythographers and philosophers of religion (e.g., Rudolf Otto and Nathan Söderblom) for tracing the origin of religion to a discrimination of the sacred from the profane, for placing the apprehension of the Divine at the center of the religious conception, and the emotion which the Divine produces at the center of worship. Man, who has a predisposition for the Divine, rises to the intuition of it by means of the stimulus given by the unfolding of the universe before his admiring and awe-struck gaze. But the external stimulus does not create the idea of the Divine; that is within man himself, like the idea of the beautiful, the good, the true, and the absolute, not derived from the senses but innate.

Like instinct, like the secret force of will and intuition, like the apprehension of a musical composition which eludes the more subtle intellectual analysis, the charm and mystery of the Divine are outside the range of reasoning. It would be vain to embark on the laborious task of clothing in another garb that which must, because of its nature, remain unknown—vain, because our attempts to make it clear to the mind, so far from simplifying, as most people erroneously suppose, in reality complicate and distort our apprehension.

Religious emotion in Judaism, then, so far from depending on an intellectual perception of the Divine, is really dependent on experience of a quality that is felt as inherent in the religious object and makes us perceive it as something quite different in kind from anything else. And, as it is impossible for the intellect to make it any clearer, the experience of the Divine must be said to be irrational. This experience—unlike the suprarational, which is divorced not only from all intellectual definition but also from all emotional experience—produces, in those who are predisposed toward it, certain specific emotions, which cannot be confused with other similar emotions or be regarded as mere summation of those usually experienced.

William James, who certainly rendered good service in analyzing religious facts from the point of view of feelings, acts, and experiences, thus advancing toward a region which lies beyond the rational, still made the mistake of not observing that religious feeling, which is qualitatively distinct from any other, is not a mere name given to a summation of a series of feelings.

It may indeed be more correct to assert that the religious feeling is a specific reaction in the presence of something which is perceived as sacred; and in cutting religion clear from all dependence upon myth and all heterogenetic development of mental images and feelings, one may be linking it up (as Schleiermacher once attempted to do) on new and more solid foundation to its own roots, which go down deep into the irrational region of the human soul.

No one has yet carried the analysis to the point of being able to isolate that original complex which, in order to distinguish it from the Divine into which intellectual and ethical elements enter in due course, is termed the "numinous" by Otto. This complex, which is perceived under different aspects—now as something enchanting, overwhelming, endless, stupendous, sublime, and even as something awful and terrifying—is what sustains both religion and magic, and constitutes that common basis for both which has very frequently led to their being mistaken for each other, especially in the early beginnings, where the conclusions of historical observation and psychological research are more uncertain.

This basic element continues in successive cultural developments to struggle with the doctrinal and ethical superstructures and with the eternal effort, which has not yet completely succeeded, of disassociating religion from magic. But if we remember that the original experience of the Divine is not the equivalent of that religious feeling which is both richer in ethical and intellectual content and tends constantly toward the acquisition of ideal values, and if we omit from our consideration that first critical moment in which the whole of life through the whole range of its manifold activities is struck by an impulse which shakes it from its very roots in every direction and in every part—then we realize that the phase which the experience of the Divine represents in the awakening of the soul to prayer, although essential, is yet not the one and only phase.

The revelation of the numinous to human consciousness is the first note which the Divine strikes on the strings of the soul, and the soul is thrilled with its harmony and intoxicated with all its light; but the revelation of the numinous cannot yield that particular ethical covering of the Divine which is conspicuous by its presence in the prayer of the great religious geniuses. The experience of the numinous is, rather, a revelation of a basic original complex by which the genuineness of every revelation of the Divine that is subsequently perceived can be tested. But it is in its turn preceded by a vital impulse, which is not, like the numinous, perceived by individuals, but acts from the depths of the irrational, like an organic prime mover directing every movement and development of all living beings. This is experienced by everyone in every energy which sets life free within the wide radius of its possibilities.

Although the experience of the numinous is necessary to the religious life, just as the experience of truth, beauty, and goodness is indispensable for the creation of science, art, and morality, yet it is by the vital impulse that man is continually urged forward to triumph over pain and death and that the great mass of humanity reaches the same goal. Beyond this goal, few, very few, succeed in penetrating into the secret temple of the numinous. Urged on, as all are, by the impious necessity which leaves an indelible mark on every religious act, it is only the experience of the numinous which, like a mysterious star, guides their eyes toward the regions of the inaccessible and the incomprehensible. But it is the vital impulse which gives rise to those particular functions of religion and prayer which the simple experience of the numinous would never have been able to obtain.

In order to understand this vital impulse, it will be sufficient to reflect that no one appears to be more completely the creature of limitations than a Jew. Enclosed within a world of contingencies, of whose threats he is at first inclined, in the instinctive interest of self-preservation, to be more conscious of himself rather than of the world's resources, he seems condemned to hammer unceasingly on the bronze walls of the prison which contain his destiny and his glory. It contains his destiny because a Jew cannot live unless he is enclosed within a horizon, unless he is subject to empirical limitations in space and time, nor can he raise himself unless he agonizes in the effort to do so. It contains also his glory because the limitations that weigh painfully upon him and the work of overcoming them are necessary alike to rid him of indifference and apathy and to render possible, with the victorious exercise of power, an increase in his worth.

Virtue and heroism are tested in danger, and it is only through the continual effort to become better, as Cromwell said, that men become good. In art, the vital impulse shows itself by opening out perspectives, by robust reaction to the painful labor of realizing an idea that always lies beyond the attainable; in science, by the struggle against the unknown; in ethics, by the struggle against evil; in religion, by the desire which calls for the conquest of the emphemeral and contingent world through the stern task of reaching whatever cannot be grasped, of discovering the enthralling mystery, through the ineffable joy of attaining the Divine.

The hold which evil has upon human nature is strong and deep. But no less strong is the impulse for liberation and victory, which at one time works itself out in the empirical world, occasionally taking the most tragic forms; at another time withdraws into the stern silence of the conscience, where forgetfulness threatens at any instant to sever the present from the past, the uncertain hope from the morrow, the ephemeral effort from the present; where a vain endeavor is made to arrest the moment that is inevitably passing. And only by stepping forth heroically to press on toward the unattainable, only by the undying impulse to shatter the bronze walls of his prison, can a Jew lay hold of the material for building his own glory.

Such, in brief outline, is the function of the vital impulse, which, starting under the sting of pain and the experience of evil, moves toward a greater power, a wider domain; an impulse which, almost inevitably, drives every thinking Jew to find an instrument and an absolute guarantee for the attainment of liberty and victory.

In Judaism this infallible instrument is represented by worship, in its threefold Covenant form of charity and righteousness, atonement, and, above all, prayer. But when a Jew has found in prayer not only a means of triumph or a source of comfort but also the way which leads him to freedom, to the

Divine, he has arrived at those peaks from which a new and much wider and richer horizon stretches, beyond the confines of the irrational phase of his religious awakening.

The Rational Phase of the Awakening

So far I have considered the irrational phase of the soul to prayer—the vital impulse which stimulates it to the most varied functions in the life of the spirit, and the experience of the numinous, which sustains its characteristic and unmistakable emotion. We now undoubtedly find ourselves in a position, somewhat better than before, to understand the nature of the peculiar relationship which prayer expresses, especially if we bear in mind that the vital impulse by no means exhausts itself in activity whose sole objective is the preservation and expansion of the material life.

It operates not merely in instinctive flight from those dangers, such as famine, persecution, war, sickness, etc., which give frequent occasions for the outburst of prayer; rather, as I have already said, it surrounds and stimulates the totality of life in all its forms and expressions. Neither confined to material interests, which exhaust themselves in the possession of what is of use for the organic life and its preservation, nor yet confined to the practical objectives of the psychic life, the vital impulse extends also to what is desirable in itself, to what is an end in itself, and therefore to ideal objectives.

This fact is particularly important for investigating the origin and nature of prayer, especially now that in certain Jewish philosophical and religious circles the opinion has become very general that religion, and especially prayer, is exclusively devoted to practical and secular ends. It should, however, be easy to understand that since that craving for mystery and liberty which produces prayer is tending in a given direction, it requires for its development a wider scope than that of a simple affirmation and expansion of the physical life. Nor could the gradual rationalization of the visible and invisible world, which is so necessary for the development of the religious conscience, be conceived unless there existed that interest in theoretical speculation on the first and final causes of things which the various cosmogonies, mythologies, and theogonies reveal.

This means that the activity of the spirit is not confined to an instinctive process of preservation and a biophysical expansion, which is in itself irrational, but extends also to the higher activities that constitute the practical, theoretical, and ideal values of the spirit. The origin and growth of the sciences, the arts, and religion would not be intelligible on any other supposition. And it means that prayer is not a pure and simple expression of the instinctive interest in preserving material existence, but is also an expression of spiritual life extended to interests of a higher order.

We may interpret in this sense the answers given to G. F. Moore, the American psychologist who, some years ago, asked several persons of a certain degree of culture what it was that they sought and found in religion. These answers, though differing in form and wording, might be summed up as the expression of a single desire and a single aspiration—life, more life, a life more intense and richer in content. Prayer will in fact, at each stage of its development, preserve this characteristic: while not neglecting in any of its phases the needs of a physical existence, and while not quitting the irrational basis from which it springs, prayer will always be found to be the only rational instrument capable of liberating, redeeming, and transforming man; transforming and renewing him internally by bringing him to the Divine and uniting him with it.

If prelogical thought developed to account for the logical and moral absurdities that were especially frequent and conspicuous in primitive mentalities, this hypothesis has nothing to do with the irrational foundation of the religious activity. It would, moreover, be inconsistent with the fact that this activity is never completely separated from the rationality by which it is destined to develop. Prayer, as I have said, arises from a vital impulse and from an experience of the numinous, both of which are essentially irrational; but one must not forget that, functioning as they do through the life of the spirit, religion and prayer, insofar as they are consciously directed to clearly defined aims (and we have no instances of civilizations in which they are not so directed), are obviously rational. It does not in fact need further argument to show that prayer is really an instrument which is considered on rational grounds to be adequate for the attainment of those blessings which the worshiper seeks.

The rational and the irrational are, therefore, phases in one and the same development, not two stages, one of which precedes the other and is in some way independent of it during the course of the development of prayer. For as soon as it has arisen from the vital impulse and the experience of the numinous, prayer enters inevitably into the framework of rationality which surrounds all manifestations of the practical and theoretical life. In fact, at each stage of its development we find these two phases in which prayer reveals its hidden origin and its glorious end.

It is not so with the hypothesis of prelogical thought—a hypothesis which definitely marks off a period of insensibility to logic from another period during which that sensibility arises. For if it were true that the primitive mentality does not recognize causal relations except as relations of position and juxtaposition, as Lévy-Bruhl supposed—it being of entire or comparative indifference whether one of two given points came before or after the other in time—primitive prayer would then no longer have any meaning for life.

In this connection various examples are usually quoted, such as that of some savages of North America who took an eclipse of the moon to be the explanation of a massacre which they had suffered some years previously. According to Lévy-Bruhl, the eclipse ought surely to have preceded and not followed the event. But in this case, apart from the fact that we should take care not to make the mistake of generalizing and drawing from one example a conclusion that affects practically the whole of primitive mentality, it is certainly not clear how, even to a primitive mentality, a sign that is given afterward can explain the reason of events that have already happened. It would be more reasonable to regard the error of those savages not as depending upon the absence in them of the notion of causality, but rather as derived from the belief that human events have some connection with the movements of the heavenly bodies. There are, in fact, many inconsistent and immoral practices which are due to erroneous beliefs, such as those relating to the contact with taboo, to the evil eye, or to sympathetic action induced by magic. But when we see the primitive mentality devoting itself to the scrupulous observance of obligations and to avoiding any breach of the laws which govern the social and individual life, we cannot but recognize a continued application of the principle of causality, and at the same time a continued attempt to confine the attention to the scrupulous observance of obligations without scrutinizing their content, especially when it is a question of religious obligations.

What in fact strikes us is that these obligations, associated as they are with emotions, with lack of practical activity or with mental inertia, and due as they are to imitation, to habit and above all to the subtle suggestion or tyrannical action of the community, tend to paralyze the rigorous application of logical thought as well as the examination of the moral content of the obligation. It is this failing that renders it possible for the Bororos to consider themselves not men but "arare" and for the Indian Coda to see God himself within every grain of corn. But we find an abundant supply of similar instances even in those religious faiths which are considered the most advanced, though it never occurs to anyone to pronounce the modern man insensible to logical contradictions and to the principle of causality. Theology, with the authority of a thousand years of agreement behind it, has only to declare that logical contradictions are supernatural truths, has only to condemn the denial of this as sinful, and at once every believer has sufficient reason to suppress every attempt to submit these affirmations to the scrutiny of common logic.

The specious theory of Emile Durkheim according to which the principle of contradiction depends on historical and consequently social factors, must be considered erroneous; unless by the term "historical factors" is meant the habit of accepting as suitable for collective action, without examining their implications, things that are logically contradictory. Such, for example, is the case with contradictory attributes assigned to the Deity itself, sometimes by means of religious syntheses. The synthesis of the beliefs of conquered peoples with those of the conqueror and their subsequent combination in what is often a somewhat haphazard system can only gradually and in part triumph over the original chaotic mass of religious beliefs and practices by eliminating one after another of their contradictory elements.

But what has not been sufficiently borne in mind in the history of the rational systematization of prayer, of religious rules, and of worship is that many of their contradictions depend to a large extent on precisely this irrational phase of religious development.

Those who, in the discussions about the relations between philosophy and religion, have brought out the fact that religion must always contain a secret world, veiled by a mystery which can only allow man to catch glimpses of the Divine but never to reach and fully grasp it, have already recognized that the field of religion is not coextensive with that of rationality. Religious knowledge therefore, rejecting all analysis of the objects of worship and faith (since these can be only imperfectly presented) and of worship itself, creates that habit of mind in which no believer troubles to concern himself with the question whether this faith and his religious actions are logical or not.

Thus we find that a mythical person may sometimes be represented as a mortal, sometimes as an immortal, as a man or as a woman, as a contemporary or as the offspring of his own father, without thereby raising in the mind of the believer any sense of outraged logic or any feeling that a position so plainly self-contradictory requires explanation. It is enough for him that he finds in religion that numinous quality that cannot be ascribed to the profane world and before which he bends in adoration.

It would, however, be a mistake if, from this peculiar position of the religious world, we tried to extract an insensibility, even on the part of primitive mentalities, to such fundamental principles of logic as those of causality and contradiction. It is sufficient to cast a rapid glance over the religious life of primitive peoples to find in them the same instinctive confidence in their own memories as in the uniformity and regularity of the process of external events. This confidence is clearly based upon the principle of causality and it enables man to seek and to find suitable and effective remedies for escaping from pain and obtaining what gives him pleasure. It enables him also to find in religion the guarantee for arriving at his desired destiny.

If primitive man had really lived in a prelogical stage, he ought to have stopped at every step and to have passed from one state of wonder to another every time that he saw water run or the sun rise; and if he had not believed that certain causes constantly preceded certain effects, he would not have been able to defend himself from dangers, to guide his movements, or to resort to prayer to attain the object of his desire. We see that man has always employed the methods of comparison, variation, and association, and has taken for granted the uniformity of nature, as John Stuart Mill taught; moreover, man has employed the principles of induction and deduction as well as of causality and contradiction, though often abandoning them, especially where religious traditions and the duties of believing were concerned.

History does not offer, and could not have offered, any example of a cult which does not rest upon a certain systematization of knowledge. On the contrary, a cult cannot be conceived that is not preceded by an interpretation, however rudimentary and mistaken, of the unseen world and at the same time of the instrument which is employed for getting into relation with it. Far from leaving us to conclude that we have to do here with insensibility to the logical or ethical sense, this mistaken theory should, rather, lead us to recognize the presence of an irrational phase which man, with his instinctive need for rationalizing, continually but in vain tries to explain away and eliminate, employing that well-known potent instrument of research—intellectual demonstration.

Until we limit prayer to the vital impulse and the experience of the numinous, we have only a simple cry of the soul, astonished or frightened or disturbed or fascinated in face of the tremendous mystery, in face of the inconceivable, the wonderful, the unnamable, the terrifying, the ineffable. Until we conceive of prayer as religious dread, as the flame of divine yearning, as an expression of fear or alarm, awe or anger, hate or sorrow, affliction or joy; or, better still, until we see prayer within the compass of a simple affirmation of the will to live, the buds of reason grafted onto *reason's* trunk will be few and hard to find. But as soon as the characteristic emotional expression of prayer brings with it a certain consciousness of the limitations of human nature and a radiant hope of obtaining by its means the object of the heart's desire; as soon as it requires belief in secret powers or in beings conceived anthropomorphically, to whom a desire can be addressed (prayer, properly speaking, means desire), we see many buds of reason already growing on its trunk, the fruits of which will in due course ripen in the light of the logic of thought and feeling—a light which, though not always clear, is yet always present.

I said above that, before word and action (the sole means man possesses for communicating with others) are employed in the specific form of prayer, there must already have been some working out of knowledge and of feeling and some classification of them, thus giving rise to a conception of the effect which prayer can produce and the energies to which it can give free play, and at the same time a conception of the nature and character of the forces with which man, when he prays, seeks to get into contact.

From this we may draw conclusions which have a wider bearing than would at first appear. We have seen how it is that the irrational phase and the rational phase, or rather, the coinciding of these two essential phases of prayer, will never cease trying to capture and rearrange its impulses and its experiences under symbols, images, and allegories; the constant labor of portraying the unportrayable, conceiving the inconceivable, and grasping the unattainable; the ardent yearning to transcend, under pressure of the vital impulse, the boundaries which divide the finite from the infinite—how it is all these produce and maintain prayer.

Prayer will always bear the indelible marks of the motives and the occasions which create it, of the necessity which the vital impulse lays upon it, of the human effort, of the mystery which the experience of the numinous brings. But its history will nowhere show it to us as a pure and simple expression of its two phases, the irrational and the rational. Both these phases will always continue to sustain prayer. The irrational will offer constant resistance to every intellectual and ethical elaboration and superstructure; and they in their turn will try with equal constancy, but in vain, to crush and efface it or at least to drive it back to the earliest stages of human development. The most logical attempt which the history of human religion has been able to show, amid these wearisome struggles to make the unapproachable and the incomprehensible fit in with the rational viewpoint, has perhaps been that of the Hebraic conception of the Messiah, a conception which, by incorporating into prayer man's highest ideas of human perfection, has, in anthropomorphic fashion, humanized the Divine but also has divinized man. This point has not been appreciated by the philosophical criticism of religion; but it is precisely this inherent presence of the irrational element in the idea of religion and in prayer which gives birth to the contradictions and paradoxical manifestations that, if we interpret them (as some have tried to do) merely as survivals of illogical superstitions, will remain utterly inexplicable.

9

The Significance of Irrationality

Irrationality is not the highest philosophical concept, for it is merely an expression of a relation of the external world to observing and suffering men. It is neither a thing-in-itself, nor does it find a place in a metaphysical world-picture; it belongs either to a sensualistic, psychological, or at most to an epistemological world-picture. In spite of this, the absurd is among the most important perceptions to which the thinking Jew can attain of the relation of the outer world to himself. The irrational and the absurd are not only of the greatest interest to us theoretically, as mental products, but they also have an enormous importance for the sphere of practical life. There are, of course, profounder orders of ideas, apart from purely theoretical speculations concerning the Absolute, and so forth. Even with respect to ourselves, there are profounder expressions, but these are entirely academic. Nevertheless, our life is overarched and overshadowed by these gigantic negations, as by an immeasurable specter, and for us there is no escape from their gloomy domain.

Irrationality also indicates the incongruence of the universe with humanity, for irrationality is in evidence more in the sphere of perception and thought than anywhere else. An enormous number of appearances in the external world may be grasped through our intellectual activity, and for these many different names are at our disposal. We therefore say that they are intelligible, meaning that they are intelligible to us. Among them, for example, are the causal principle, the principle of the conservation of energy, and so forth. But here, where the point at issue is that we observe only qualities and changes, which correspond in grammar to adjectives and verbs, here begins the sphere of epistemological irrationality; for after deeper reflection, we come to the conclusion that for us the so-called things, which in grammar correspond to nouns, remain completely inaccessible, and that we have only appearances. To this sphere also belong deliberations concerning the noetic value of the primary experience of transcendence, the overvaluation of which leads to solipsism, and concerning the value of the sensualistic experience, which, if we do not proceed critically enough, may lead to dogmatic materialism. All false problems and antinomies of the concept of infinity, the problem of subject and object, the body-soul problem, the questions and contradictions as to the meaning of the universe, and finally, all higher and more general conceptions; above all, the great neutrals, not to speak of the transcendents, unknowables, absolutes, and so on—all this is partly or wholly incomprehensible to us. We are justified in admitting our ignorance or inability to know in the face of these problems, and in speaking of an epistemological irrationality.

It is incomprehensible that this irrationality should be obvious in proportion to the coefficient of *ignorance* in most *Weltanschauungen.* In a sensualistic world-picture, however, there are many things to which irrationality is not functionally related. It is otherwise in the epistemological world-picture, where we are fundamentally unable to escape from the admission that we cannot grasp the true essence of things, and are limited to appearances. In a fictive world-picture, this is even more obvious. And if the thing-in-itself is unknowable, so of course is its theoretical and speculative superstructure. If the thing-in-itself is a limit-conception, in which light vanishes and darkness begins, then that which is postulated behind the thing-in-itself lies eternally, of course, in the very deepest obscurity.

Nevertheless, with respect to the metaphysical world-picture, which must be imagined as completely transcendent and relationless, we cannot speak of *irrationality,* which always expresses a relation to *us.* There is no bridge to lead us into this world-picture; nothing that concerns us has any validity in the relationless, metaphysical transcendence.

Practically, therefore, one may recognize two irrationalities:

1. The epistemological, which consists in this, that for us the theoretically postulated pure object remains unknowable. Here we are defeated at once by this brief statement of the *inability* to know.

2. With respect to the phenomenal world, it consists in this, that we perceive and recognize much that is entirely without meaning, order, or coordination, or seems to be so; that we are forced to assume that many things would appear otherwise if the world were the work of some kind of intelligence similar to our own. With respect to this second irrationality, one may still distinguish further:

a. We may hope that in the future we shall come to understand much which today seems without order, and that in many spheres we shall introduce the order now lacking. For example, there is the hitherto entirely incomprehensible gulf between the empty and the full, between dead matter and life, between the animal and the human intelligence. Into all these abysses, it is quite probable that in time we shall be able to throw so much light that they will cease to exist as such, and that our knowledge with respect to them may be welded into a homogeneous picture.

b. But the contradiction that the universe is conditioned otherwise than we human beings expected, by which I am referring mainly to the impossibility of approaching the universe with moral demands, must in the future become still greater. In ancient times, there was no contradiction. By superficial observation, Plotinus could still grasp the universe as "cosmos"; the superstitious Middle Ages could comprehend the world known to them as directed by a humanly thinking Providence. As a result of more profound observation, we receded further and further from the notion that the world is anthropomorphous, parallel with man, and exists only for man. Let us invert a saying of Francis Bacon's: superficial knowledge of the world leads to God, profound knowledge leads away from God.

Summing up, one may say that irrationality in the sensualistic world-picture must lead to the avowal of human ignorance, and to the more emotional and more painful recognition that the universe does not respond to human, moral, and other requirements. The first negation may be slowly mitigated with the progress of human knowledge; the second, of a more fundamental nature, must be permanent.

One might perhaps be tempted to speak of irrationality as of a principle. Whether one chooses to do so depends on the sense which we give to the word "principle." If we mean by this word the accentuation of a very general mode of thought, much as we are accustomed to speak of principles in natural science, as of quite generally valid forms, the use of this word with respect to irrationality can be justified. The case is altered if we wish to grant to the concept of "principle" a sort of metaphysical validity or metaphysical background. Here we must be on our guard. Nothing would be more erroneous than to promote a purely generalizing thought-form to a sort of supersensual metaphysical positive.

I will take the standpoint that in the depths of the universe there exist many different intelligences of which our humanity represents only a special case. To every one of these possible, indeed probable, intelligences something different in the universe will seem displeasing, strange, unparalleled, irrational. Even if we grant that the judgments of these hypothetical beings will agree in some things, there is nevertheless a much wider area in which every intelligence will reveal a separate subjective interpretation, dissimilar from the rest.

We will grant that certain things affect us as though they must represent themselves to every intelligence observing the outer world as almost equally intolerable and irrational. It is obvious that by far the greater majority of these irrationalities, which may perhaps have common sources in the longing for individual happiness, the desire for personal authority within the framework of the environment, and regret for the presence of unjust sufferings, must appear beyond all measures diverse and manifold if they are regarded from a common standpoint and compared with one another. Hence it may be said there is not one fundamental irrationality, somehow always the same, referring to all cases in a similar manner, but rather a vast mass of irrational-seeming individual experiences to which we must ally the term irrationality merely as a collective name, without expecting more from this name than we are accustomed as a rule to expect from general conceptions. General conceptions are not real; they merely serve the very human need of orientation in the external world.

If we wish to consider a single instance of irrationality in a rather more concrete manner, we discover a situation which may be expressed by the sentence: a straight line and a curve are not parallel. We human beings always want a straight line, and nature is always curvilinear. We want *one* prime number, nature wants *another.* But prime numbers have no common measure.

But if our human experience does not agree with reality, with the pure object, if we are not satisfied with the world-picture offered to our senses, this nonaccordance is never a principle in the metaphysical sense of the word, but a perfectly harmless otherness, whose basis is not in any way higher or deeper. An otherness which is always more probable than similarity and always represents a more general standard is an otherness which seems to us the more harmless and innocent, the more we are in a condition to disregard our painful human interest in knowledge, in truth, and in the external world.

Thus the alleged principle of irrationality has melted into a mere more probable indeterminacy, irregularity, disorderliness. Nothing can be otherwise than it is; disorderliness is always more general, more probable, than a uniformity, than an order operating according to our human notions. It would be a monstrous, improbable case if instead of this indefinite irregularity and disorder everything should consist of beings exactly like men. Just as though a thinking triangle or a thinking circle were to expect the whole external universe to consist merely of triangles and circles. Such a case must appear all the more probable to us in proportion as man is the more complicated in comparison with the simplest geometrical figures.

Also, irregularity is only a human, epitomizing term for a series of observations, among which a definite relation prevails which does not correspond with an expectation. But, strictly speaking, this irregularity does not exist; it is only a human collective name for a great multiplicity of individual things. There are only dissimilar but compared appearances, and the objects presumed to correspond with them. Thus in a higher sense there is neither irrationality nor any principle of irrationality. Irrationality is only a human, summarizing word, an expression for the disillusioned human perception in the direction of the totality of being. It exists only in our minds; it exists only for us human beings. What is outside man is only an otherness, a difference or, rather, enormous numbers of "otherwise" formed, changeable, different individual appearances, not to be reduced to a common measure.

I arrive at the conclusion that irrationality somehow exists only for us; it is, humanly speaking, a very unpleasant business, for which, however, no one—least of all our Creator—can be made responsible. We must bear no malice because the world behaves irrationally with respect to ourselves. There is nothing left for us but patience and resignation.

Despite this state of affairs, we are still justified in asking the question: What causes may lie at the root of this irrationality?

As we human beings are constituted, we must understand appearances in such a way that they cannot occur without a presumed pure object, because they form the synthesis of this object with the perceiving subject. The thing-in-itself seems to us in a certain sense a concomitant condition of the appearance, even though we are aware of the metaphorical quality in this word-sequence, since we must not without more ado transfer the known causal connection from the sensualistic world-picture to the "in-itself." We must not so far forget ourselves as to postulate a sort of metaphysical irrationality.

Irrationality resides neither in God, to which some of our perverse brothers should like, of course wrongly, to transfer it, nor in ourselves, but in their conjunction, very much as though the two basic elements of human thought were somehow unable to tally.

Irrationality in the sense of the unknowability of the thing-in-itself appears to us, then, as agnosticism, which is an epistemological and by no means a metaphysical principle. As to how things look in a room whose doors are closed to us, I can say nothing. "Closed doors" are the symbol of irrationality and agnosticism.

It is perhaps needless to mention that in the more superficial irrationality of *appearances* there can of course be absolutely no relation to metaphysics. Irrationality here resides only in individual things and individual appearances. It is true that the whole prospect of the universe, with its hyperabundance of inanimateness and vacancy, in which we cannot perceive any sort of purpose, has a confusing effect upon us. This is, however, only the first impression. On closer observation, the total view of the universe disintegrates into a series of microscopic processes, which are to be explained individually, and of which the majority can be explained.

The anthropomorphic conception of the universe in religion—in short, theism—or even the still more sublimated deism, cannot explain this so simply. For these *Weltanschauungen* the principle of metaphysical irrationality, which I so abruptly rejected in the above exposition, must be called in to explain the universe. Indeed, they need more than a principle; they need a person. And since the world-explaining tendency of religions usually includes in itself a moral order, they cannot but have recourse to a moral, immeasurably wise Person, whose existence, of course, excludes all irrationality and purposelessness. If, for example, the universe is ruled by a wise and moral being, it is likewise wise and moral, and our great denials have no place in it. In this case, one must speak of Providence, of the all-wise decrees of the Creator, and so on.

If this does not work, if evil cannot be argued out of existence in this way, they introduce into their universe—since principles with them are persons—the spirit of evil. Theistically, irrationality and purposelessness appear as evil, as its premeditation. If a supreme anthropomorphic Reason is the ruler of the world, and if at the same time the world is a vale of tears, then this reason is an *evil* Reason. The most logical course for the theists would be simply to believe in a God who was not good. If, for example, we try to conceive and express the relation between good and evil in the world algebraically, the formula $n - p$ would be valid. N means good, p evil. The formula which would best correspond to our own known world would be the inequality $n<p$. The sum of evil is, according to our experience, much greater than that of good, so for once in a way we do not consider how crudely anthropomorphic both conceptions are. Strictly speaking, I should never admit a concept of good and evil in the usual sense. If we purge them of their all-too-human dross, so little is left that it hardly corresponds any longer to the old traditional content of these inexact conceptions. In a similar manner, one might write a formula for suffering. In this case, it would be $n = 0$ and $p = \infty$. Here, of course, irrationality and purposeless would be in the maximum of their function.

The Hebraic recognition of and belief in suffering signifies, philosophically interpreted, a sort of compromise with the evil in the world, which cannot be denied; with our irrationality and purposelessness, which then, of course, must not bear these names. Mani and Zoroaster went perhaps further than the Jews, having coordinated the two principles. If we wanted to do something like this today with respect to the existing world, we should have to allow the evil principle to be greater than the principle of good. Only a boundless sophistry could maintain and proclaim that the good principle is the stronger—indeed, that it is universal, cosmic, absolute.

In Judaism, which was burdened by the belief in Adam's expulsion from the Garden of Eden, men simply stuck their heads into the sand rather than perceive the magnitude of the principle of evil in the world. All that was maintained with respect to the reciprocal relation of God and the spirit of evil, which was always merely a way out of the difficulty, a confession of the reality, was mere verbiage, which was never thought out to a conclusion and never could be. While the spirit of evil was only a way out of a dilemma, there was yet in the "history" of suffering a will to righteousness, and indeed a foolish endeavor morally to justify God. But Jews disregarded the fact that such a justification would be possible only if based upon the principle of parity, which is absent in Judaism. In Judaism, the spirit of evil is illogical, for in its subjection to God, it cannot vindicate him.

Let me now consider the notion of purposelessness a little more closely. I have already said that purposelessness is related to the emotionally accented sphere, which is related to the sphere of perception. We human creatures long for sensations of pleasure, and therefore conclude that in an expediently ordered world there ought not to be sensations of pain, either for us or for other sentient living creatures. The concrete expression of this fantasy is the religious conception of Paradise.

In the world of experience, however, sensations of pain or discomfort predominate. An abbreviated expression for the immense number of such observations, not to be overlooked, which bear the common characteristic that the world is not ordered for us, for our necessities, for our longing for happiness and prosperity, that it does not meet our wishes, but on the contrary, brings pain, suffering, sickness, and death, is *purposelessness.*

I have already shown that there is no purposelessness as such, that it is merely a collective noun for an inexpressible multiplicity of individual things and individual appearances, which one and all follow a course to our disadvantage. It is one of the universal concepts which exist only in our minds, in order to satisfy our need for order. In a more than humanistic philosophy—that is, in the profounder regions of epistemology and in metaphysics—if there could really be such a thing, there could be no talk of purposelessness. It is a residue of the old anthropocentrism, which has been revised by the experiences of the last few centuries.

There is one thing which I should like to point out. Attempts have been made to introduce purposelessness, which has no place in the phenomenal world, into the alleged sphere of the thing-in-itself. This lower world, so the advocates of such a view maintain, is of course a vale of tears, but it is only a world of appearance. The world of true being, which is imagined immediately as a kind of Paradise must of course have an absolutely teleological and purposeful tendency.

I must emphasize the fact that this view is not the original Hebraic view in which Paradise and the Serpent had a materialistic, "naïve-realistic" existence. For long centuries, men really knew nothing about an "in-itself" in Judaism. But as it became manifest that in this world there was no place for the various conflicting Jewish views and concepts, there was rejoicing at the sudden discovery of this new place of refuge. I would like to reply to them approximately as follows:

1. By the "in-itself" I understand the pure object, unobserved by any subject; I am forced to this auxiliary hypothesis by the consideration that its contrary—that the pure object is *nil*—must lead to absurdities.

2. Concerning this unknowable limit-conception, nothing positive can or should be asserted. We have seen that the "in-itself" is not sunlike; it is no realm of light, no heaven, or anything like it, in which the positive laws other than those known to us prevail. To believe this would be to relapse into fantasies of the old Christian doctrines.

3. There is a purposelessness only in the sensualistic world-picture, where it represents a generalizing word, a superconcept, an abbreviation, in which countless sufferings of living creatures are somehow contained. In the "in-itself" there is no purposelessness.

4. Attempts to smuggle the Christian Heaven into the realm of the essential Jewish "in-itself" accordingly betray a threefold logical error: (*a*) a simply negative error of introducing an exuberant thought-form of positive content, in no way justified by experience, into a simply negative realm; (*b*) the error of attempting to introduce relations into a relationless realm of the thing-in-itself with a realistically conceived fairy-tale from the infantile age of humanity; and (*c*) the crudest anthropocentrism.

I have emphasized enough that purposelessness and irrationality are both abstractions from the perceptive world of the senses. And in this everyday world they meet with the fate of all abstract superconceptions: there are thousands of kinds of pain and innumerable feelings of distress which possess reality as single phenomena; the superconceptions merely help to orient the human intellect. The lamp "ego" throws its light into the darkness.

Human interest illuminates the universe. The greater part of the universe—a great part of our world of sense and the collective "in-itself"—remains obscure. What is not obscure is somehow disorderly; it does not range itself around us as if we were its central point; it is not turned toward us so that we can understand it, so that it may delight us. Only here and there, in our immediate proximity, some small fractions of the universe are more or less in conformity with us. How far the darkness may extend which our lamp fails to reach, into which its rays do not penetrate, we do not of course know. Elsewhere I said that this darkness is not simply nothingness, that light and semidarkness are not sheer illusion. This is the only thing I venture to say critically. But I hope that I have also shown that this darkness cherishes no hostility toward us, if only because purposelessness and irrationality do not extend to its domain, since from a higher viewpoint they have proved to be otherness, irregularity, indeterminacy, and so forth.

Should anyone object that I have merely replaced the old concrete superstitions with an abstract negation, I admit that this is so. But is it not already a notable advance to have approached in this way? Is it not enough that we have reduced the principle of transcendent purposeless, evil and suffering to nullity by means of a higher conception, in spite of the fact that we have admitted their validity for us human beings, and perhaps particularly for us Jews?

10

Probability and the Miraculous

Needless to say, all of the foregoing may be applied (in somewhat different form though with similar justification) to the problem of miracles—a subject, dare I say phenomenon, which, in recent years has occupied more and more of a place in Jewish thought, particularly in relation to, and in terms of, the "subject-matter" of the Holocaust and the continued survival of the State of Israel. It is my intention and my hope in the following section to clarify some of the often conflicting, contradictory, and obscure problems related to speaking about the "validity" of miracles. I have deliberately chosen philosophical rather than religious terms to speak about the problem in the hope that my use of a metalanguage may provide a stabler context of analysis of a subject all too problematic.

Judged by its indispensable role in our daily practical judgments, as well as in the procedure of natural science, the concept of probability is one of the most important in the whole field of philosophy. Since the failure of the romantic *Naturphilosophie* to derive infallible knowledge of nature a priori, and since the discovery that other than Euclidean geometry may be true in the physical world, it has become generally evident that all our factual knowledge (that is, all except purely formal or mathematical considerations) is probable only in the sense that we cannot *prove* the contrary to be absolutely impossible.

To an increasing extent we now find the idea of probability

developed by theologians, logicians, mathematicians, physicists, biologists, and statisticians; but, with the honorable exceptions of Leibniz, Antoine Cournot, and Charles Peirce, philosophers have given it scant attention. Possibly the chief reason for this is the uneliminatable religious and moral craving for absolute certainty, so that anything that fails to support it is relegated to the "merely empirical" realm. It is curious to note that the sharp separation between philosophy and empirical inquiry, leading to a neglect of philosophic interest in probability, is also maintained by such a thoroughgoing antisupernaturalist as Bertrand Russell.

Theories of probability, like so many other theories, may be traced back to Aristotle, who seems to have first used the word as a technical term to denote the subject of our investigation, and who treats the problem of probability under the head of "Dialectics." As a follower of Plato, Aristotle restricts *knowledge* to that which is necessarily true. But unlike Plato, and perhaps influenced by Democritus, he gives a more positive role to *opinion.* Some opinions are better than others because they are held more frequently or by those who are well informed or trained in their particular subject. If probability is not in the field of necessity it is at least in the field of law. Arguments from probabilities are thus persuasive though not conclusive. The probable is thus the problematic, which etymologically connotes a question thrown at one. At any rate, it is certain that the word "probability" comes directly from the Latin *probare*—to probe or prove. In *that* respect Locke's view of probability seems to be substantially like that of Aristotle. For Locke, also, views probability as a character of inference which lacks a basis in that which is always and demonstrably true—for instance, the knowledge that the ordinary man (not trained in geometry) has of the fact that the sum of the angles of a triangle is equal to two right angles, when such knowledge is based on the authority of those who know.

Modern theories of probability may be generally characterized as either subjective or objective, i.e., dealing with the character of our beliefs or opinions, or with the character of the objective evidence for these beliefs or opinions. Though writers on probability often more or less consciously combine these points of view, the distinction between them is in the main clear enough. John Venn's *Logic of Chance* may be taken as representative of the objective point of view, while Augustus DeMorgan's treatise on probability may be taken as typical of the other point of view, which is often referred to as the conceptualist point of view. The whole modern psychological tendency puts the emphasis on the mental phase of the beliefs called probable, and this is reinforced by popular discourse, which has many expressions for degrees of probability, such as, "highly probable," "very likely," "almost certain," "improbable," "not at all likely," and others. We say, "I am almost certain"; "I am quite sure"; "I am convinced"; "It seems to me"; etc. But the whole tendency of modern logic and exact science demands a definiteness in probable judgments which does not seem to be offered by any differences in the intensity of belief.

John Maynard Keynes in his great *Treatise on Probability* endeavored to set up as a standard beliefs that he calls rational, but apart from material evidence the concept of rationality does not seem very clear. Objective theories frequently begin with the concept of possibility, and consider the number of various equally possible but mutually exclusive happenings, but the concept of "equally possible," unless further qualified, is essentially obscure.

Events are possible or impossible. There seem to be no intermediate states between the two.

Thus probability is a category of inference that may be sharply distinguished from the kind called *necessary,* certain, or (to avoid psychological entanglements) conclusively demonstrative. An inference is rigorously demonstrable if it can be shown that it is impossible for the premises to be true and the conclusion to be false. Thus we prove a theorem in geometry when we show that it is impossible for it to be false if certain previously specified propositions (axioms and their derivatives) are true. Not all inferences, however, are of that kind.

Indeed, most inferences that we make do not take that form. Thus, that no man has hitherto attained the age of two hundred years does not prove it impossible for one of us to live that long. This *form* of inference is central to contemporary Jewish discussions of the "miraculous." Yet that is certainly evidence of a sort that cannot be ignored in science or in practice. The proposition, "All Presidents of the United States have been Protestants," does not prove that "The next President will also be one." But we should not regard these two propositions as altogether irrelevant to each other. The first is evidence of some sort for the second, though it falls short of being conclusive. We may call such inferences from partial evidence probable.

Against the foregoing view, which restricts probability to classes or kinds of inference, it may be objected that in actual usage we do mean something by the probability of a single proposition or event, that we are in fact primarily interested not in the probability of the inference but in the probable truth of propositions for which we do not know or even seek any evidence. A specific example of this is the difficult problem of miracles. Actual popular usage, however, is not decisive for purposes of philosophy, else philosophic issues would all be settled by consulting a reliable dictionary. In this case there is an obvious logical contradiction between holding a proposition to be by definition either true or false and then speaking as if probability could be characteristic of it. This attack is used most effectively by Martin Buber in his *Good and Evil.*

Yet probability, when measured, is a fraction; and a proposition cannot be fractionally true. He who characterizes a popular expression as illogical or inaccurate does well to indicate the natural source of the inaccuracy. If we contend that it is strictly meaningless to speak of the probability of a proposition, how is it that men do use that expression and are certain that they do mean something by it? The answer to this can be readily apprehended if we remember that in ordinary discourse we generally take certain things for granted and the full meaning of what we say is to be found not in the actual words used nor even in what is consciously present to the mind but, rather, in what reflection finds to be implied. Thus we speak of a body as at rest or in motion without stopping to indicate with respect to what it is at rest or in motion. If I say, "The car is in motion," we generally understand, and need not add, "with reference to the earth." We thus get into the habit of viewing the expression,

"The car is in motion," as a complete statement, whereas reflection shows that by itself it is incomplete.

Similarly we speak of "the probability of a proposition" without specifying with reference to what evidence it is probable. We may, therefore, continue to speak of the probability of a proposition, as an abbreviated expression for its probability relative to our total knowledge, or body of propositions which serve as evidence for it.

According to the "orthodox" theory of Bertrand Russell and Alfred North Whitehead in *Principia,* when the premises are true and our reasoning valid, we can assert our conclusions categorically and thus drop the "if" of the premises. Certain difficulties are inherent in this view, specifically when applied to regions where the meaning of a proposition obviously depends on the context or system in which it occurs and of which the premises are an integral part. But, however that may be, we certainly cannot ignore or drop the premises of a probable inference. For the same propositions may have different probability values according to the different sets of propositions which are offered as evidence for it. Thus the probability that a defendant in a court of law is guilty may vary in the course of the presentation of the evidence for or against him.

Keynes, in his *Treatise on Probability,* takes this relation between premise or evidence and conclusion as indefinable. Others, like Francis H. Bradley, treat it as a matter of intuition. Now we need not deny the varying force of different arguments to a mind trained in the weighing of evidence. But since all admit that probability is a matter of degree, and in some (but not all) cases measurable, it is of the utmost scientific importance to define it so as to give meaning to some criterion or verifiable way of distinguishing the more probable from the less probable. It is the great advantage of the frequency theory of probability that enables us to do this in many cases. According to this view, one class of premises defined by a single propositional function is more probable than another if it will give us a large proportion of true conclusions. And any proposition is more probable than not if the evidence in its favor is greater than that against it.

The notion of a proportion of the conclusions being true needs some clarification to remove seeming conflicts with the orthodox (and, in my opinion, correct, from the perspective of Jewish thought) view; (1) that the *consequences* of a true proposition must always be true, and (2) that no proposition, whether it is a conclusion or not, can be sometimes true and sometimes false. Reflection shows that as to the first point there is no conflict, because the orthodox rule applies only to rigorous demonstrative inference; and as to the second point, the conflict disappears when we remember that all inference, whether probable or demonstrative, is formal, i.e., applies to all classes of propositions. It is well known that the probative force of the syllogism does not depend on the specific terms that occur in it but will hold of any triplet used in a similar manner. A syllogism thus gives us a class of conclusions which are all true if the respective premises are true.

A probable inference gives us a class of conclusions of which only a part are true. Thus if there is a rule that no student of my college can be under fifteen years of age, I can conclude that to be true of *every* individual student. But if eight-tenths of all the students of my college are over fifteen years of age, I can say that there is a probability of eight-tenths that any student who leaves the building is of that age, i.e., eight-tenths of such specific conclusions will be true. This ratio will hold if for "student" we substitute "instructor," "janitor," "visitor," or anyone else. Note that there is no *necessary* inference from a proposition or premise concerning distribution in a class, to a conclusion concerning a single individual member of it. But what we can assert is the relative frequency or number of times such specific conclusions will be true if the given premise is true.

Of course our evidence may not always be as definite as in the foregoing examples. We may argue that it is more probable than not that a Jew will recover from a particular injury, because nowadays most Jews so injured recover. But we may also argue that there is some probability that he will recover even though we do not know what proportion of the injured these recoveries constitute. This, however, only means that we often rely on evidence insufficient to give us a determinate probability but enough to establish an indeterminate one.

It will be noticed that in order to use a number of observed instances as evidence for the probability of another case, we must assume the latter as well as the former to be members of a common class–else there would be no logical connection at all. For example, is a miracle a "true event"? If your child's recovery is evidence of any sort, even of the smallest weight for the recovery of my child, it must be because the two are alike in some factor that is relevant to the recovery.

This brings me to the question of the probability of an inference as to a universal proposition or "law" on the basis of a number of observed instances of it. Keynes and others have raised serious objections against the possibility of applying the frequency theory at all to such inductive inference. But these objections seem to me to apply only if we have an inadequate conception as to the logical force of induction. We must go even further than Keynes and reject the common notion–on which rests Laplace's classic formula and most theorems as to inverse probability–that the probability of an induction always increases with the number of observed instances.

Consider the usual illustration of induction given in our logic texts, namely, that of the sun rising. Is it true that the more often we have seen it rise the more probable it is that we will see it rise again? If that were the case there would be a greater probability of the man who has seen it rise 36,000 times living another day, than the man who had seen it rise 3,600 times–which is absurd. John Stuart Mill, himself the strongest defender of the claims of induction, admitted with characteristic candor that in some cases a few instances are far more probative than a much larger number of instances in other situations.

Yet surely we cannot altogether dismiss the view that the wider the experimental basis of any universal proposition, the greater its probability. What can be better evidence for a universal proposition than actual instances in which experience shows it to be true?

These conflicting considerations show that the traditional

account of the evidential force of induction is too simple and that we need to introduce some qualification or distinction.

We must, to begin with, make the obvious distinction between the initial probability of any universal proposition (which we can consider as a hypothesis) and the probability added to it when we find that its specific consequences are true. The necessity for the latter kind of evidence should not blind us to the presence of the former. Any generalization or hypothesis which, in the course of an objective investigation, suggests itself as possibly covering all the facts is likely to have some analogies in its favor or to be an instance of some more general proposition.

It therefore derives some probability from the latter. Thus the initial probability of any generalization about a newly discovered species of plants or animals would depend on the more general propositions of biology. And we always *do* start with previous knowledge *if* we wish to make progress. Thus it would not occur to a reasonable rabbi whose first three congregants to visit his study on a particular day were murderers to generalize and attribute that trait to all Jewish laymen. The overwhelming probability (or practical certainty) that all men are mortal rests not on the actual number of human deaths any of us has observed but more on certain wider general propositions about the nature of animal life. It is true, of course, that the latter propositions have a wider range of confirmatory instances; but the distinction between the initial probability of any universal proposition and that which it acquires by confirmation is still a valid one.

It should be noticed that in the very process of gathering confirmatory instances we must depend upon prior universals in order to be able to identify the instances. Consider a familiar example. An urn contains a large number of balls. They are mixed up, and I draw out a number of them which are found to be blue in all cases. I infer a probability that all are that color. All the evidence conforms to our hypothesis and there is no evidence against it. Yet we would not regard this as at all reliable if we did not know something about the constitution of collections of balls in urns, and the infrequency with which an urn containing balls of different colors, thoroughly mixed up, will contain those of a special color in just such a position as to be drawn first. Without such prior knowledge, we should be arguing from certain observations to others that we know nothing of and there is no logical magic by which we can extract knowledge or evidence or probability or anything else from pure ignorance.

The foregoing considerations will enable us to deal with the question raised but not answered by Mill, namely, why in some cases a few instances have greater weight than a much larger number in other situations. Thus one or two tests of the alkalinity of a new chemical compound may establish it with a very high degree of probability, while innumerable uncontradicted instances of white swans or pious botanists will not afford such high probability of all swans being white or all botanists pious. The explanation of all this is to be found in our prior knowledge or assumption that the color of animals or the piety of men is rather variable. The probative force or evidential value of an induction therefore depends not simply on the number of specific instances observed, but on *the degree of homogeneity of our class,* i.e., on the extent to which instances or samples are typical or representative of the whole class. Concerning miracles, the problem posed in this way should be thoroughly clear. This point is of the utmost importance in guarding against the fallacy of selection.

Suppose I examine a large number of Jews and find that they have certain characteristics, say, certain peculiarities of diction. The inference that all Jews will have that trait is subject to the fallacy of selection. All the Jews examined may have been of a certain social class, or of a certain geographic location, or my particular mode of questioning them may have helped to bring about the particular response. My generalization is then not true of Jews as such, but rather, of any people belonging to a particular class or location, or responding in certain ways under certain conditions—so that other Jews will be altogether different.

If I think of such possible alternative explanations of the result, I will use the methods of agreement, difference, and concomitant variations to test my generalization. But if I do not know what factors are relevant and responsible for the result, and rely on a large number taken at random, I rely only on the hope that special circumstances will not operate in all my cases. A large number may therefore not be as probative as a smaller number subjected to critical tests. That is why statistical or purely empirical formulae or laws do not have as much weight in science as those that are rationally derived.

We may thus conclude that the probability of inductive inference depends on two factors: (1) Every generalization which does not comprehend the entire universe is an instance of a more general proposition that may have a certain probability or be known to be true in a number of instances. To this extent, the probability of an induction clearly conforms to the frequency theory as applied to the quasi-deductive examples used above. (2) Though confirmatory instances are always needed to meet possible doubt of our general propositions or of those on which it rests, no number of actual instances observed, or not observed for that matter, is sufficient (in the cases of unlimited classes) to give us a determinate probability.

For we cannot by mere numeration tell what proportion of the totality is constituted by our finite collection. Instances alone can in such cases give us at best only an indeterminate probability, and there is only a barest minimum of scientific value in showing that a certain proposition is barely probable, i.e., not impossible. What is of greater value in scientific procedure is to show that any generalization or hypothesis has a greater probability than any of its possible rival alternatives; and this is achieved by showing that it holds in a greater number of properly *comparable* cases.

I have hinted before that the great advantage of the frequency theory of probability is that it enables us to give a definite account of how to verify probability theorems as well as miracles. The latter is a great desideratum in view of the loose way in which the term "verification" has been generally used.

According to the traditional Talmudic accounts, Jews verify an alleged miracle when its consequences are found to be confirmed by sensory experience. (Seeing is believing, but touching is the naked truth.) This mode of reasoning, however, is the well-known fallacy of arguing from the affirmation of the consequence. And it seems rather scandalous for theology to maintain such a double standard, condemning an inference as a fallacy in the part called deductive and glorifying it as verification in the part called inductive. We may of course remove the scandal by insisting on the distinction between proof and verification. When offered as a conclusive proof for the truth of the antecedent, the argument from the affirmation of the consequence is a fallacy; but when offered as a verification or as evidence of its probability, it is relevant and generally the only means of testing its truth. But even so, a realistic account of verification must take a relativistic form and envisage not a single hypothesis which can be verified by confirmation—a task too "easy" to be of much theological value—but, rather, a process of weighing rival miracles.

If we have two or more competing miracles and we can make a crucial experiment or observation which confirms one and disproves the other, then the one that is confirmed has thus been demonstrated to be a *better* account of the facts so far known. Verification, in other words, does not strictly prove a miracle to be true—the history of Judaism (to say nothing of Christianity) shows well-verified "miracles" to have finally turned out to be false—but it gives us a logical reason for regarding one as more probable than the other, since it explains more of the facts.

The prevailing account of verification contemplates universal propositions that predict certain uniform results and exclude others as possible. They can therefore be refuted by a single instance to the contrary. But this does not apply to propositions that assert a probability. If, following James Maxwell and Ludwig Boltzmann, we assert that the probability of a cubic centimeter of gas dividing itself into two distinct parts of unequal temperatures is less than one in a quadrillion, the actual occurrence of such an event will not constitute a refution of our assertion. For the improbable is not ruled out as impossible.

We are thus tempted to draw a sharp distinction between the verification of laws such as those of classical mechanics, on the ground that no crucial experiment or observation can refute the statement of a probability. If, however, we consistently adhere to the frequency theory, we realize that the test of a probability statement requires not a single observation but a large number, since probability judgments are directly concerned with groups of phenomena. If the particles of a gas did frequently divide themselves into two parts of different temperatures, we should have a right to question any theory which assigns this occurrence such a low probability.

If a penny falls head forty-nine times in fifty throws, we may well question whether the proper probability of all its falling head in any one instance is one-half. According to my analysis, to assert the latter is to predict that it will fall head as often as tail. This is a material assertion which must ultimately rest on experience, and it would be absurd to contend that what has been affirmed on the basis of past experience cannot be denied on the basis of further experience.

On the theory of fair dealing, it is extremely improbable that my opponent will hold four aces twice in succession. When that actually happens, the hypothesis of fair dealing is not refuted; but we may well reconsider it, and entertain the contrary one as a more satisfactory account of the situation. We certainly would do so if that hand were repeated more often.

It may well be objected that this way of verifying a probable miracle is very imprecise, that it offers no definite canon of telling when a run is sufficiently long to serve as a test. Abstractly stated, this objection is certainly sound. But we must not forget that the actual choices between mechanical hypotheses which make universal assertions—for example the choice between the Ptolemaic and the Copernican astronomy, between the corpuscular and the wave theories of light, between the continental and Michael Faraday's theories of electricity—were not as easily decided by crucial experiments as the popular theories assert. Despite Lavoisier's experiments, the phlogiston theory continued to be held for a considerable time, and Galileo's supposed refutation of Aristotle's theory of gravitation by dropping two objects from the tower of Pisa is rather mythical, for under the actual conditions of height, atmospheric friction, etc., such an experiment could not have been decisive. Science, like theology, in fact, depends on cables of many strands rather than on chains of many links. It is wise, therefore, to insist on the real and important distinction between the verification of universal propositions and the verification of assertions of probability, but also to guard against making the distinction too sharp.

It may be urged that when we speak of the probability of unique events, we do not think of classes of events, but of the individual case. But what does it mean to think of an individual case? If our thought is rational, it seeks reason or evidence for the given event. If we find any reason or evidence, its force will apply to any indefinite number of instances similar to ours. If I reason that Moshe Dayan is a patriot because all soldiers are, the force of the argument does not depend upon the peculiarity of Mr. Dayan. I can replace Dayan with Cohen or any other individual. Any *Z* is a *Z*, if all *X*'s are *Y*'s and all *Y*'s are *Z*'s. The rational force, while felt in a single case, cannot be restricted to it. There is, therefore, nothing strange in saying that while we speak of the probability of single events, the logical or rational force of our statement has to do with certain features of it which are essentially repeatable. The unrepeatable individual, indeed, is not the subject of science and certainly cannot be expressed in language.

Finally, it is urged that when we apply a general rule to an individual case we have, at best, only a probability that the individual case does conform to the general rule, and that this probability cannot be explained on the frequency theory. The true force of this objection can be seen if we realize that it holds for all deductive arguments. If I say that all electrified bodies repel each other, this is an electrified body, etc., the judgment as to this body is a *salto mortale.* It rests upon evidence which can never be conclusive. Now the probability of a premise does not affect the certainty of the inference, though it does affect the conclusion. Most of the objections to the relative frequency theory of probability are significant only if we ignore the context and ground of scientific knowledge. Otherwise, the only alternative is to accept the frequency theory as the best exemplification of what we mean by probability. But we must not forget that, technically, probability may be indeterminate.

It is curious to note that in the realm of religion and metaphysics, where prevail the greatest differences of opinion, almost all parties are agreed in *rejecting* the notion that knowledge in these matters might be only probable. But it is obvious that our knowledge of the absolute totality of things or of an omniscient and benevolent Creator, whose nature is beyond our powers of imagination, cannot be demonstrable knowledge in the ordinary sense of knowledge and proof. The various proofs for the existence or nonexistence of, for example, God and miracles, rest upon principles which appeal to certain minds, but which others can question without disbelieving in logic. The modern tendency to question self-evident principles can certainly not be excluded from these realms.

But the reflective mind cannot stop with so-called empirical knowledge, for the more we reflect the more uncertain become the assumptions on which our empirical judgments rest. The drive to consider that which is beyond the merely actual is at the basis of not only all human activity but of all efforts to understand. In that sense, metaphysics is not an additional realm, but something implicit in all rational endeavor.

Traditionally, metaphysicians thought that if they could find something permanent and self-evident they would have the key for the understanding of the totality of the world. Modern reflective philosophers are not certain that any such key is to be found, and are highly skeptical as to whether we can treat of the totality of things under the same categories as we treat other objects of rational consideration.

What kind of a world is it of which judgments of probability can be validly asserted? For if the mind includes everything, the statement that probability exists in the mind only is meaningless, and if there is some reality other than the mind to which its ideas must point or conform, then the question remains as to what earthly or unearthly relation ideas can have to a world which is radically different from them.

If probability is a genuine trait of the world in which we live, the latter contains many objects, patterns, configurations, or abstract aspects which are indefinitely repeatable in certain ratios or proportions, and this means a world in which not all things are possible, but some things are impossible. If the actual world is thus a selection from a number of possible ones, actual objects could have been arranged in different ways without ceasing to be intelligible. And this means that there is, in the world, an element of contingency which is radically undetermined.

I have noted elsewhere the error implied in the common assumption that the reign of law, such as physical science proclaims, requires absolute determinism. On the contrary, if there is a genuine plurality of atoms, electrons, or any other units which determine each other according to invariant relations, there must be, by the very hypothesis, some distinction between the existence of any one thing and the influences which operate upon it. We cannot, as Jews, believe in a world of functions without anything which functions; in grins without cats. Ultimately, the world is what it is, and logical necessity can only be the derivative from certain characters which happen to exist or to be.

Contingency can never be eliminated, no matter how general law may be. The attempt to derive existence or nonexistence from mere concepts is doomed. Moreover, the world is more than relations of order; and of course, it is vain to attempt to describe that which is beyond all relations and predicates. Surely no description of what we are can be exact and completely exhaustive of our actual being, and this must be true of any world in which there is a genuine plurality and a genuine Creator.

11
Philosophical Knowledge

Our most valuable ally in the region of relatively reliable forms of knowledge, wherever the epistemological aspects threaten to become one-sided, is psychology. Of possible forms of knowledge, that of critical realism is probably nearer to the truth than that of idealism, because, in spite of the accepted working hypothesis of an external world transcending our consciousness, it is, after all, that which does least violence to our common sense. But I should be the last to maintain that this modest science can suffice for all our needs. I have no intention of dispensing with Kantian epistemology.

I cannot, in the long run, believe that we are alone, that there is nothing outside ourselves, not even external impressions, but that even the "primary experience" of transcendence occurs in some way spontaneously. And these are the consequences of condemning the psychological (realistic) prejudice. If I am not to think anthropomorphically, and abandon, for example, the belief in substance, I must not carry criticism so far as to land me in the cul-de-sac of solipsistic nihilism. But here I am doubtless expressing an epistemological prejudice; for every man, to be sure, can assert the realistic prejudice: *c'est moi!*

Psychology *alone* would lead us to take altogether too superficial views, but the psychological outlook is just as necessary to the all-too-speculative epistemology as is the research conditioned by this science to its unassuming sister science.

Psychology is modest, unexacting, and purely descriptive, but therefore capable of evolving. It shows very clearly how man, from his primal, animal origins, has slowly attained, by the road of passive reflection, to ideas, and by the road of active reflection, to conceptions.

For psychology, many of those problems which cause philosophers of pure consciousness so much perplexity do not exist—such as the problem of the second person, the problem of time and space, the problem of affinity, the problem of the cause of sensual perception, and so forth. The collaboration of psychology and epistemological criticism is the collaboration of the senses and the intellect. The relation of these two components depends on the thinker. It is possible that the thinker who esteems psychology, hence experience and sensualism, more highly, will be more likely to adopt the objective standpoint in philosophy than one who regards the intellectual components—reason and epistemology—as more important, and is consequently inclined to adopt the attitude of the philosophers of subjectivity.

Analgous to this relationship between psychology and epistemology is the relationship in science between the descriptive doctrines and mathematics. Hence in the history of human thought two schools may be demonstrated. One is based more on the intellect and its reflective activity, which would like to recognize an absolute human knowledge, and is generally inclined to dogmatism. In this school, we should include Pythagoras, Plato, the medieval Scholastics, Hegel, Husserl, and the modern phenomenologists, structuralists, and philosophers of pure consciousness. The second school is based on the experience of our senses and natural science. It has been from the very first less severely orthodox, not averse to the notion of the relativity of human knowledge. To this belong Democritus, Epicurus, Bacon, Locke, Einstein, most medical and scientific men, and the modern philosophers of objectivity, logicians, and logical positivists. This second school has always been regarded as slightly superficial. I do not think it has ever been justly estimated. It has always been the school of the physicians and the physicists, just as the other has numbered more priests and jurists. The scientific school has relied upon experiment, observation, and discreet induction, and has admitted that there are an infinite number of things that must forever remain inaccessible and incomprehensible to humanity. It is of course true that today there are even some philosophers of pure consciousness who practice strict criticism, discretion, and reserve with respect to new conceptions, especially positivistic conceptions. But these are exceptions, and only quite recently have there been such exceptions. Their predecessors were very different. Until recently it was the rule that radical skepticism, despising all human knowledge, all objectivity, lay claim to an alleged higher knowledge in those spheres in which, after the critical rejection of the world of objective facts, only the blackest negation should have existed. All sorts of fantasies were introduced in regions where, after the expulsion of the despised science, only negation should have reigned, and thereby the door was opened to the blackest obscurantism. The second school, of course, often appeared superficial, and tended toward materialism, but it never lapsed into such obscurantism.

In my own view I should wish as far as possible to combine both aspects and offer a synthesis based on the mutual criticism of the two systems, and endeavor to go forward on this hypothesis.

The psychological standpoint is increasingly influencing human subjectivity. We have a psychology of thought, a psychology of *Weltanschauungen.* Only from the standpoint of psychology can we clearly understand why there should be such great differences in the region of *Weltanschauungen,* and how many thinkers have so organized their inner life that they incline to follow a definite direction. Only this science can explain, for example, why Susanne Langer thinks so highly of figuralism, why Hans Vaihinger has made the concept of the fictions the central concept of his whole system, why Herbert Spencer proceeds from evolution, and why Hans Mautner perceives the fundamental defects of our mental development in the imperfection of our speech. Only psychology will explain why other thinkers overestimate the primary experience of transcendence and see such high walls between it and the rest of the psychic life. Every editor thinks it proper to preface the works of a philosophical author with a psychological analysis of the philosopher. From this analysis it should be obvious why the philosopher in question had to develop just these and no other views, why the fabric of his system had to acquire just this and no other subjective coloring. In science such a procedure is not necessary. In philosophy the deeper we penetrate the more necessary it becomes. Of course, the more critical the philosophy, the more skeptical, the more given to negation, the less it searches for the Absolute, the less necessary will it be to resort to psychological explanations.

But psychology is important not only for the personality of the thinker, his characteristics, and his hypotheses; we need it also for the criticism of philosophical thought itself. If today we discuss a great philosophical conception, we must first of all give the history of its origin and development on a purely psychological basis. We cannot continue to assert that psychological knowledge is too humble, that it offers us only experience and nothing higher. Indeed, if experience is reasonably combined with epistemological criticism, it gives us the highest stage of knowledge which enters into practical consideration. It is a question whether there is a still higher knowledge, and, if there should be a theoretically higher one, whether it is nearer to the truth.

Many of us believe, for example, that the recognition that "we must all die some day and shall be dead for all eternity" is on the whole of great value to us, although it is based only on experience. How can it be refuted? From the empirical standpoint, by nothing whatever. In the so-called higher stages of knowledge, of course, it can be refuted by the explanation that eternity is an illusory concept derived from the concept of time, and only an intuition form of our intellect. In reality no such thing exists. The primary experience is timeless, and only that is absolute. Thus there exists, even in a higher knowledge, no time, no death, no eternity, no past, no future; just as no external world exists. I am afraid, however, that this alleged higher knowledge is no nearer to reality.

It seems to me that it is very difficult to defend this higher knowledge. We have seen that there can be no such thing; but to reject on this account the basic hypothesis of our spiritual life in time, space, causality, and so forth, without irrefutable reasons, and to assert that there is a higher being in which they do not exist, seems to me incorrect. We get no further with the everlasting repetition that our knowledge is not complete. Is there a higher knowledge? Perhaps. But of what kind is this knowledge? Can we maintain that this knowledge excludes, for example, the time-and-space concept? I do not venture to assert anything of the kind. Any other, higher knowledge than the human is merely thinkable, not imaginable. Any attempt to represent the content of this knowledge is, from a critical standpoint, merely to build castles in the air.

I assert as strongly as I can that the continued existence of the world after the death of any individual person seems to me so important a point that although logically and critically and epistemologically it cannot be easily defined, it nevertheless deserves that one should erect a philosophical system on its basis. This very point, which cannot be eliminated from the world because it is always being newly confirmed by daily experience, shows that there is some object without my individual subjectivity, or without any subjectivity, and that the index of consciousness does not include the entire object in itself. There are also things outside our consciousness of which we must agree that they still *are,* insofar as it is possible to employ that terribly eleatic verb *to be.*

I might summarize what has already been said in the following manner: the everyday experience that through the death of any individual subject the enormous world-picture of the objective world does not cease should be reckoned among those fundamental cognitions which allows us to suspect that the philosophy of pure consciousness is a modern movement, which began with Bishop Berkeley and Immanuel Kant and carried through to Edmund Husserl and his successors, and to which, in the development of human thought, only a theoretical validity is to be accorded. The thought-forms created by it are theoretically, of course, unusually valuable, and one must not overlook it. But its importance will be overestimated if one labels it as the unique truth and rejects the opposing epistemological considerations. The philosophy of pure consciousness assumes, in the history of human thought, a high but not the highest rank. It is an aspect among other aspects. Epistemology, of course, ought to purge and fertilize all special scientific and philosophical provinces by its criticism, but it can never be responsible for a positive enrichment. Our consciousness offers knowledge a colored glass, whose influence upon the world-picture always retains its relative value, if only because we have nothing better to put in its place.

Our epistemological world-picture, gained from the standpoint of objectivity, which, with the results of science, will be comprehended in a coherent whole, will never degenerate into philosophical radicalism (as the contrary opinions are compelled to do), even though its tendency is critical and skeptical.

At the close of this chapter, my reader will probably come to the conclusion that I have actually approved of most attacks on the world-picture of naïve realism, and have declared myself in accord with their destructive activity. But I do not associate myself with the final attack, which, if I take the standpoint of modern scientific and philosophical knowledge, I may regard as repelled. I do not believe in substance, matter, or the possibility of absolute knowledge; I do believe, however, in something outside my consciousness, in respect of which individual subjects might come to an agreement.

I think it will save some trouble to summarize the major points of my argument.

1. Above all, I do not regard the standpoint of dogmatic, or even of methodical, solipsism as providing an adequate aspect for critical philosophy. The fiction that we are quite alone in the universe leads in its further consequence to absurdities. For me it is as good as decided, even though it is not epistemologically demonstrable, that besides my ego there is also a nonego; that is, the external world and other subjects "exist."

2. The external world consists for me in appearance; nevertheless, I am compelled to have recourse to the auxiliary concept of the pure object, that is, of the thing-in-itself, whether one employs this name for the reality transcending our consciousness, or whether one makes use of another designation. The thing-in-itself is to be understood as my agreement that something appears to me in some way. It is incorrect to speak of a causal connection between the thing-in-itself and the phenomenon as if it were the cause of the phenomenon. The

causal connection is here only a *form* under which these things appear to me, but whose metaphorical character must be always emphasized.

The "thing-in-itself" does not "exist" in the sense of naïve realism, as if it could ever be an object of observation, and one must not introduce anything positive into it. Still, one must not assert that the "in-itself" has a metaphysical existence, whose feeble echo is the maya of appearance.

The Platonic metaphysical essence is to some extent a higher quality; the "essence" of naïve realism, the "in-itself," does not stand above appearance. Any evaluation is out of place here, and even if one admitted it on principle it would be methodically incorrect, since the thing-in-itself is an enchanted Sleeping Beauty, which no Fairy Prince can kiss awake. The moment he kissed her she would become an appearance. The kissing Fairy Prince is, of course, the perceiving subject. What the Sleeping Beauty is for us is forever unknowable.

3. "In-itself" is an object without subject, an airy vision, which, to whatever kind of subject, is forever inconceivable. The only positive thing about the thing-in-itself is a kind of double negation; namely, that it is unthinkable to imagine the subjects alone without the help of an object.

4. We must recognize the validity of the time-and-space conception not only in the psychological, but also in the epistemological, world-picture. If one consciously goes out of his way to consider the problem of the "in-itself" of these concepts, one should take it to be a synthesis of subjective and objective moments, and not a creation of pure consciousness, not a mere imagining.

5. In both conceptions there are many negations: succession is as inconceivable as simultaneity: the time sequence does not permit of reversal. In this respect, space signifies less than time; spatial relations are reversible, and the most different kinds of space are conceivable. Euclidean space is only one among many. Time, however, is one and the same. Perhaps I may express it in this way: In the time conception, our intellect could not have introduced so many moments of subjectivity as into space. Time must be more to the "in-itself" than space. I am here, of

course, speaking only metaphorically; I wish to express a probability, not to make a confident assertion.

6. Apart from space and time, which represent only directions and relations, but not things, and, further, possess neither "substance" nor "existence," as we are naïvely accustomed to assume, the external world consists of antecedents and coexistences, which we learn to grasp as qualities and changes. In these qualities and changes, there is—humanly speaking—apart from a great number of "irregularities," a certain exceptional "regularity." *We* are of such a quality that of the rich abundance of happenings, much appears to us as regular, but much as the contrary of regular. From the standpoint of other imaginable intellects, there might be rather more or less regularity. But for us it is very difficult to imagine that nothing outside the perceiving subject corresponds with these regularities and irregularities which signify the order and disorder of qualities and changes, even if we have to concede that the so-called order may be nothing else than our image of the external world, which we and only we have created for ourselves out of many other possible images.

7. The universe cannot be known by means of our speech: that is, by means of our thought. Speech originates from a time when man still thought of the world as quite small and simple. Speech is sensualistic; it corresponds with naïve realism, which was properly a materialism.

8. In appearances and relations we always remain only on the surface. We describe only changes and qualities. The "in-itself" is only postulated.

9. It is beyond our capacity to decide (*a*) when we really do *not* know something; (*b*) when spurious problems confront us, among which, of course, are the so-called ultimate problems. What we "do not know" we shall perhaps know in the future. It is the essence of the spurious problem that its insolubility is inherent. Properly speaking, it does not exist.

10. The insolubility of ultimate problems is shown in this, that intellectually we must admit that affirmation and negation occur simultaneously, which leads to antinomies. Sometimes we cannot assert even this. Sometimes we are compelled to form

sentences between whose subject and predicate no definite relationship exists.

11. Our world-picture is something like a temporal eternity and a spatial infinity, or something nearly approaching to it, which for the most part is empty. The vacuum in space is immeasurable compared with the filled areas. Man has long been the victim of the infantile yearning to animate the universe: that is, to interpolate something egolike or anthropomorphic in our notions of the external world. This personification was the work of an imperfect intellect, and the subconscious human desire to transfer all kinds of abstractions—such as activity, purpose, and meaning—from the sphere of the little to that of the infinite. This leads to endless confusion, since we animate most of all precisely those things in which there are no physiological preconditions of the psychic life, or where the psychic is contrary to reason.

12. Since the universe is almost empty and almost dead, but not entirely empty and not entirely dead, it is entirely improbable that *all* our conceptions of the external world are merely maya. Here and there perhaps our notion of the external world may have some analogy with reality. We cannot, of course, know where. Beyond the observation of certain regularities, of a certain order, which we grasp to some extent with the help of time, space, and other relations, we can never go.

12
Jewish Knowledge

There are two points of departure from which we may attempt to ascend the epistemological summit in Judaism. One way leads from within ourselves, from our consciousness, and experiences the external world of our senses as something secondary, sometimes as something nonexistent. The total external experience is interpreted as the contents of consciousness. As to what these contents of consciousness may be (if anything), and what corresponds to them, apart from our ego, there is of course a great difference of opinion. Most of the philosophers of Judaism who employ this epistemological method feel that the character of immanence must be ascribed to our experience, and equally to all which it communicates to us of the alleged external world (by this, of course, is implied the experience of Torah as well as of history); that the questions with regard to the origin of *ha-Shem* are falsely stated, and are based merely on the so-called realistic prejudice, which unfortunately dominates the modern intellect.

This view is the more important inasmuch as it is shared by an ever-increasing number of living Jewish philosophers. Here I can only remark that the point of departure from the deepest kernel of my Jewish ego, from my so-called "primary experience" of Yahwist revelation in Torah, permits a theory of Jewish knowledge only in terms of a solipsistic method. Whether you and I openly accept this, or whether we make use of a circuitous route, of some other conceivable connection, we should at least, for the time being, consider the hypothesis that there is nothing else besides our ego (Jewish), nay, that apart from the momentary present there *can be* no past and no future for a believer in Torah. There are, of course, various ways in which the method of the solipsistic Jewish present can be built up, completed, extended, and deepened (not the least of which is an analysis of Jewish guilt, or unjust suffering); taking guilt as a basis, for example, one may arrive at various conclusions. But if solipsism is a possible point of departure for a Yahwist philosophy, which profits by its methodical advantages in its ethical structure and its mode of expression, the traces of the manifold violence which solipsism does to natural Jewish sentiment cannot be effaced. Every Yahwist philosophy must sooner or later be entangled in difficult contradictions, or abandon at the outset the attempt to give us an asnwer to the most important questions.

My Jewish mode of *Weltanschauung,* and my way to redemption, proceeds then from this starting point of solipsism, but is modified at once. I desire, first of all, to regard the world surrounding me, the world of senses, quite objectively, and *for a time,* not merely to forget that according to most philosophers of Judaism, the world-picture formed by our senses as against the "primary experience" is not only something secondary, but something much less "real" than the "primary experience": I will also forget, at the beginning of my examination, that all the senses "communicate" about the external world; I consider them to be merely the content of consciousness, and, as Kant would say, they may merely be appearances of something in itself unknowable.

In contrast to the solipsistic point of departure of other Jewish philosophers, the term "materialistic method" seems to force itself upon me. It seems, namely, as though at the outset I shall have to avail myself of no philosophy, but simply a kind of naïve realism with a strongly materialistic flavor.

This designation might perhaps be justly applied to the beginning of my efforts, for materialism is always valid for the practical life of mankind as a whole, so long as mankind is not occupied with philosophy, but lives, as it must, chiefly in order to be able to live. But I would be misleading if I were to tend toward dogmatic materialism, which, of course, is as far removed from any philosophy of Judaism as from the philosophers who set out from other assumptions.

I shall deliberately regard the world of perception, *for a short time only,* as though we could trust our senses and our intellect, but only in order to gain a *point of departure.* If we were to reject this *Weltanschauung* entirely, we should throw away resources of exceptional importance—the results of two thousands years of human investigation—the only thing which can be intellectually controlled, and concerning which it is possible to reach an agreement now and then.

If we did not take any account at all of the colossal achievements of the natural sciences, we should be no better off than the Greeks of the so-called "late period," who, without the resource of empirical science, endeavored to oppose the invading superstitions of the East: an attempt which, owing to the scientific (to say nothing of the spiritual) defenselessness of the time, was doomed to failure from the outset.

I will not generalize to the extent of saying (though there are certainly few exceptions) that the one-sided application of traditional Jewish philosophy, which throws away in a lump most of the results of scientific research, and by its partial but therefore apparently effective skepticism thrusts aside the results of empirical research as a whole, tends toward reaction. I will not anticipate: I will only glance at the mentally shackled thinkers of the Hellenistic period, who, in spite of the brilliance of their philosophy, remained in intellectual darkness. In the later intellectual history of Europe, there arose the figures of the medieval Scholastics, and of Hegel, and, last but not least, such characteristically modern thinkers as Max Scheler, Franz Rosenzweig, Martin Buber, etc. We are experiencing today a remarkable efflorescence of traditional Jewish philosophy, a contempt and depreciation of science and its methods, and a notable revival of the so-called occult sciences. That our modern age can no longer impose upon us such heavy intellectual fetters is not due to the merit of the above-mentioned philosophical thinkers: but since we have passed through periods of mental freedom and high attainments in science, it is no longer possible to return to developments of this kind, as might incidentally be expected after many of the mental manifestations of our time.

If I have no great inclination to linger over the starting point of Jewish philosophy, the "primary experience," and consciousness, this is because of my conviction that it is precisely the most primary psychological facts which are least under control, and that because of their subjectivity and insusceptibility to control they can but rarely be clearly grasped. There floats before my mind something like this: one dreams, one has feverish conditions, hallucinations. The bystanders gaze on the sleeper, the feverish patient, they note all the objective symptoms, his rapid irregular pulse, the condition of his heart, his eye movements, and so on. But what of the pictures that pass before him in his dream, which are not observed by the bystanders—are they a reality? From the standpoint of some of the Jewish philosophers of consciousness, there is no dividing line between dream and reality, as we distinguish these two conceptions in normal life. Can we, however, retain this standpoint for any length of time? Must we not say something like this: that in everything subjective, everything psychical, there is a much greater coefficient of illusion when it is still theoretically so immediate, so "primarily experience"? Is it not likely that other reasons may be adduced which make it inadvisable to build up our world-picture entirely on a foundation so insecure?

If I were to look further for a more suitable name to describe the philosophical views set forth in this chapter, I would much rather employ, instead of the discarded word "materialistic," a designation which is negative indeed, but far more in correspondence with the fundamental character of the ideas developed. I suppose I should call it a nonpragmatic and nonhumanistic philosophy of Judaism, the antithesis of a philosophy that regards man as only a highly differentiated creature.

If I speak of a philosophy of Judaism in terms of a nonhumanistic philosophy I, of course, am well aware that I am guilty of an intentional exaggeration. For I am really writing of a path, a direction, a method, an attempt; of an endeavor which, strictly speaking, must be frustrated, but which yet attains its object, even though doomed to failure. I would most gladly escape from the inevitable humanism, from the anthropocentrism so constantly emphasized in philosophies of Judaism.

This nonhumanistic philosophy of Judaism should be so constituted that man does not play the central role in the world in which he puts his faith—a faith which from a biological standpoint is both necessary and useful, but which in any theoretical deliberations must give rise to an erroneous optical attitude, which may, however, be avoided through a more critical comprehension. But excessive humanism has not only the defect of seeing man as the central point of the universe, upon which everything turns: from the human standpoint, it sets too high a value on man himself, and regards him solely from its subjective aspect.

I am of course aware that in the strict sense of the word there is not and cannot be a nonhumanistic philosophy of Judaism, that the terms correspond to a false or spurious conception: as though man could possess a scientific mentality and a mode of philosophy of other than a human character, derived from no human sources. I have always considered Goethe's dictum, "Man knows not how anthropocentric he is," as one of the profoundest truths uttered by that great thinker. Man cannot think otherwise than humanly, and a great part of his knowledge is humanism. Further, this knowledge partakes of the forms of humanism current in his age and in the country in which he lives. The fact is too little considered, that we proud Jews of the twentieth century are really not so far advanced. How large a mental legacy from the dark Middle Ages, what a great and dubious inheritance from the Stone Age, still haunts our spiritual life. We are hardly able to conceive for ourselves the spiritual condition of a Chinese or an aborigine, to say nothing of presumably higher and different forms of intelligence. Being so formed, we must be well aware that our profoundest thoughts can only be a humanism of the twentieth century, which later centuries will have every reason to contemplate from a higher level.

Thus Judaism cannot really desert the sphere of humanism. If nevertheless I have chosen such a daring designation for my world-view, I have done so in order to document my intention; for a consistent standpoint (i.e., consistent with a philosophy of

Judaism which refuses to confine itself to the facts of the conscious processes alone, and accepts the existence, in some form or other, of some kind of external world of perception indefinable according to epistemology, to say nothing of metaphysics) can be realized only if we do our best to isolate the observer from the thing observed. Man must be aware of his subordinate position in the universe; for this must impress itself upon him as a result of the achievements of natural science. If he leaves the ground of natural science and ascends to meditations upon epistemology, the platform won by preliminary scientific work must nevertheless have a permanent influence on him, guarding him against philosophical one-sidedness.

A nonhumanistic philosophy of Judaism will also save him from the judgments of value of the kind made by theologians who judge ethics in terms of "situations." In practical life, man can hardly avoid making judgments of values. Such estimates are based upon the pleasure principle, which again is anchored in biological assumptions. Above all we have to live. The difference that one object is edible and another not, the circumstance that air is indispensable for breathing and thus for life, and so on, guides the first man to a judgment of values. Pain, hunger, and thirst (and nausea, too, for my wife is pregnant) must be banished, and their opposites will be desired. But since we still estimate value so childishly on occasion—as for example, when we consider the right hand worthier than the left, over worthier than under, the lion and the eagle worthier than the dog and the sparrow—estimates of value will certainly be out of place in a critical, philosophical work. Nor should we regard animals and plants from the standpoint of their utility or malignity. We must not compare the glowing mass of the sun with the substance of our brains, and esteem the small brain of greater value in comparison with this enormous mass. This kind of estimate accords with the old, biologically explicable egoism of the human race. It proceeds from the view that all that exists is for man. This egoism, in its turn, is responsible for our more or less naïve expressions for the purpose or meaning of life. In this sphere assertions have been made in the past which Jews need not recall today. Apart from wholly medieval notions, it strikes

Jews as odd today if we hear, for example, the preservation of the human species, or the spiritual uplifting of the world, described as the *end* of creation. From the human standpoint such views are comprehensible. They should never be brought into relation with such extensive conceptions as, for example, Torah, *ha-Shem,* etc., which belong to another chapter of the history of thought than those extremely ancient conceptions of the "everyday" human life which arose in the struggle for existence.

A nonhumanistic philosophy of Judaism will set us free from anthropomorphism and anthropocentrism. And although it will not "work" quite satisfactorily, it will at least persuade us to think that man might not form *the* central point of world events, and also to reduce to a minimum the personification of the powers of nature, a mental habit of which we cannot entirely cure ourselves. We must not permit ourselves to think of the world as a magnified Jewish ego. A nonhumanistic philosophy of Judaism frees us from a Theism which *is merely inherited,* and also from the belief in so-called substance, and from any overestimate of the personal ego which we refuse to elevate to a principle of creation.

But in another respect, also, it is possible for us to approach the nonhumanistic world-view. Let us be critical with respect to our language. Let us realize that it still carries along with it a large stock of words which have arisen from an old, childish form of thinking, which presented the whole world and its events as narrowly related merely to our inner selves, in some fashion akin to our ego. There are many such words, and it is no small merit of our Talmudists that they have drawn our attention to many of these verbal corpses. There are words which remain only words, long after their original connotations have disappeared.

I have examined what a nonhumanistic philosophy of Judaism is *not,* and should not be. I have discussed which way it should travel. But I have not determined where it ought to lead us, and what final result it should envisage.

Any critically constructed doctrine of Jewish *Weltanschauung* is today subject to so many restrictions that it ought not to surprise us if its conclusions are perfectly barren and utterly depressing. If we would approach the "higher or deeper" spheres of reality, if we would strive to come nearer to the truth—or what we Jews call the truth—our world-view can in the last resort be no more than a perfectly reasoned agnosticism: an admission that our mind never can and never will penetrate the ultimate ineffability of *ha-Shem.* If we cannot bring the surrounding world under a common denominator; if our critical mind is able to work only within certain "lower or superficial latitudes," and if even then its operations are restricted, we must come to a definite agreement. The spheres of what Jews consider knowledge which are swathed in the black veil of resigned ignorance are gigantic compared with what we *can* know, and what the intellect has the power of appearing to know. This vastness of the unknowable can be otherwise expressed. Perhaps the positive declaration that it is gigantic, and in this way unknowable, says too much. Perhaps we should be satisfied to say that we can learn something of only a little area of the enormous unknowable, without saying what we ought to think of this unknowable. The higher we progress, the blacker, the more negative will everything be, and the more notes of interrogation will lie in wait for us on every side. In the world of resignation literally everything vanishes.

I shall not for this reason deny that there is progress in our everyday life. There is truly progress, and it is good that there is. But we remain always, only on the surface: we know what we want for life, but we do not want to know much. Now and then we realize the abysmal depth of many philosophical problems. They are not only insoluble, but often it is not even established whether they *are* problems, or whether they only seem so to us. Great and profound questions do not permit of being thought out to the end. It is not easy to speak of *ha-Shem,* the Absolute, and I might even say it seems to me a blasphemy to do so, if I could only rid this word of its pietistic and rabbinical flavor.

My conclusions will restrain me from speaking of the Absolute, or indeed of absolute truth, or of absolute value. It affects me painfully, as though I were listening to myself as a child speaking with other children in a kindergarten, when these combinations of words are used. To this category belongs the common manner of speaking about the meaning and purpose of the existence of the world, or of the Creator. It is almost a matter of good form with many philosophers of Judaism to say a great deal about such thoroughly illogical and impossible combinations of words. Children like to hear them.

From this it follows for me:

1. A nonhumanistic method will furnish a broad, comprehensive picture of the world, which is for the time being entirely unphilosophical; and also, from the standpoint of naïve realism, provisional, monistic, materialistic, physical, and for the time being vulnerable to every epistemological criticism. This picture, of which the *temporary* character cannot be sufficiently emphasized, should of course be traced only in accordance with methodical considerations.

2. In the second stage, this picture must be elucidated to some extent, in the sense of the empirical-critical method, by epistemology, so that the weakness of *merely* physical observation and naïve realism may be fairly exposed. Then, at this stage, a philosophical world-picture may be drawn, for the most part negative in character, but which, since we are still true to our fundamental attitude, will not vanish completely in negation.

3. At last, of course by way of suggestion, an attempt must be undertaken, on the basis of a refined and critical epistemology, to lift the *Weltanschauung* further into the metaphysical heights, where, of course, only blackness, negation, and silence reign.

Thus one ends in more or less complete agnosticism. Into this all other philosophical views of Judaism debauch, provided they are critical. Even the consistent philosophy of pure consciousness must end here. That we know nothing about *ha-Shem,* and shall never know anything, is the final sentence of every philosophy of Judaism which deserves the name. But we shall still be psychologists to this extent, that we must set a certain value on the *way* to the highest and deepest realm of darkness.

I have not chosen this method for the sake of a final,

resigned admission of ignorance. I believe that on the path through the objective world, which admits of some control, our world-knowledge—at least in the intervening stages, which are, practically, the more important—can be given such a form as will enable it to hold its own before competent criticism in a still remote future.

Epilogue

The Problem of Secular Judaism

"Secular Judaism" is an embarrassing term, which owes its origin to the fact that some Jews were unwilling to surrender their ancient and enormously valued concept of God even though they were aware both of the contradictions inherent in it and of the impossibility of bringing it into harmony with modern scientific and philosophical thought. Logically, secular Judaism is a *contradictio in adjecto,* just as though one were to call a great ocean-liner a fish or an airplane a bird. The term suggests a belief in an impersonal principle, to which one gives an antiquated, personal name that is absolutely emptied of content. In the seventeenth century Spinoza, for example, was still obliged to use the word *deus* while thinking *natura,* lest he should be burned alive as a heretic. Today, however, this is a superfluous precaution as well as a crude logical error. Here what is impersonal has at the same time to be a person, which must always be thought of and endowed with a species of ego sentiment.

Any contradiction in the term and the concept was explained away by the sublimation of the second part of the combination: in other words, by employing the God of Israel no longer in a literal but only in a fluid and indefinite sense; whence results an entirely superfluous tautology: a sublimated God-concept.

To attempt to conceive of the difference between the God of the "beyond" and a God of a world which is a metaphysical nothing is an intellectually tortuous exercise. Even speaking about God from the standpoint of a sensualistic transcendent presents intellectual difficulties, although in commenting upon it the secular Jew is moving in familiar waters. With the separate stages of the epistemological transcendence, the difficulties are still greater. But at all events it cannot be denied that the secular Jew believes that he can still to some extent appease himself by establishing the difference between the God of Torah, who is negative indeed, because unknowable, though necessary, and a metaphysically conceived nothing.

But the secular Jew encounters the worse difficulties when he attempts to compare metaphysical concepts. Here he is confronted by a transcendence in considering which, against all human possibilities of imagination, he has to think of God as absent, in order to make Him metaphysically relationless, and also a metaphysically imagined nothing. No doubt the difficulty here described is a spurious problem, but one should not pass over it in silence. The secularist fares badly with any systematic recognition of the higher kinds of transcendence. He cannot escape from intellectual difficulties and contradictions.

For some modern Jews it is sufficient to define Judaism as that sociological reality in which Torah ethics is supposed to be presented, but more than this is not allowed. In practice, among those who hold this view, the synagogue, for example, is usually described more in terms of its function than of its traditionally understood nature.

This is the characteristic understanding of Judaism by those who are vaguely designated as Jewish liberal theologians. Judaism, their argument runs, should primarily be a society of Jews acting as an ethical leaven within the larger society as a whole. Judaism is not, according to this view, an organic historical entity, but a social contract, and Jean-Jacques Rousseau and Thomas Hobbes are its prophets. Individual freedom of faith and democratic government are basic to its principles, and no indispensable connection between one's personal faith and his membership in a community of faith is recognized. Such, briefly, is how the problem has been regarded by Jewish liberalism of this century. Being very nearly obsessed with the application of Torah ethics to immediate social problems, many liberal Jews have simply substituted a "social Torah" for *mitzvot.*

Upon this concept of Judaism, or *Judaisms,* the liberal finds it both anomalous and fruitless to base an unfavorable criticism of the divided state of Judaism as a whole. Judaism must inevitably have divisions in the modern world; for since the essence of Judaism is a purely sociological quality, the argument runs, Judaism must conform largely to the society of which it is a part. Jews in these "units" are permitted to feel a common bond with all other Jews, a feeling which may satisfy them as an expression of true fraternity; but no theological significance may be attached to such a feeling in the sense that it expresses a unity belonging to Judaism's very nature, a unity which is disregarded or threatened by denominational and secular Judaisms.

Those who regard Judaism's unity as a thoroughly spiritual quality are not the only ones who fail to be distressed by the existing state of division of Judaism into the Judaisms of Orthodoxy, Conservatism, Reform, Reconstructionist, etc. There are some who positively welcome these divisions as a necessary and desirable characteristic of modern Judaism. Some argue that the very strength of Judaism depends, paradoxically, upon these divisions in theology and practice. Where there are no theological divisions, the faith of Jews becomes complacent in its self-sufficiency, the argument goes. The tension which is sustained by opposing doctrines and interpretations keeps Judaism in a healthy state of unrest, for it demands that beliefs be constantly proved and checked. The view is: let us continue to be divided, so that a kind of Jewish faith or at least a kind of Jewish practice may abound. When this secular idea is proposed as a rejection of the uniformity of Jewish religious belief, it commends itself to those who will not equate uniformity with unity. Even in the areas of modern Jewish thought where "consensus Judaism" is most genuinely realized, there are differences in theological interpretation. But these do not necessarily threaten the unity of Judaism so long as they are not allowed to disrupt the faith of other Jews.

The danger of this position is that it is easily capable of being perverted—and often is—being changed from a defense against theological stagnation to a pragmatic rationalization of divisions based upon issues which are not strictly theological. In the past, differences in theology have certainly stimulated the intellectual activity of Jews, but they have also been used as wedges to drive people apart, making cleavages which are partly theological in nature and partly social, moral, and political. Moreover, when problems of theology cease to be living ones, when they become petrified as unalterable dogmas to which assent must be given as a condition for recognized legitimacy in Judaism, and when they defy all challenges made by opposing interpretations, it can hardly be claimed that the welfare of Judaism is being served by such divisions, nor that its unity and coherence are not being jeopardized.

Confronted by the theological, liturgical, and social differences which do exist between the major segments of Judaism in modern America, some persons have been satisfied to explain the lack of outward unity by what may be called the "branch theory." According to this view, which commends itself to many fair-minded Jews, the prototypical Torah-believing Jew is a tree having different branches which, though distinct, are still part of the whole.

Logical as the branch theory may seem to be, it has been opposed vigorously by those who have a less accommodating view of the contemporary proliferation of Judaisms. The theory stands for a conception of tolerance which owes its origins not to the Torah, but to modern humanitarianism; and its main weakness is that the question of Judaism is isolated from the question of truth. In other words, the theory does not take seriously enough the belief that the unity of Judaism consists of other factors than common heritage alone. What *is* our standing ground if we take the familiar line of ascribing to the Orthodox, the Reform, the Conservative, the Reconstructionist, etc., their special attributes and functions within an imagined organic totality? However democratic this commonality of heritage may sound, it is hardly Jewish theology. Where Jewish unity is concerned, therefore, many authorities believe that the existing branches are to be judged, though not necessarily explained, on the basis of theology rather than sociology. And the theological understanding of the people of Israel does not seem to allow for the claims of the branch theory.

The emphasis upon fixed boundaries, moral relativism, voluntary membership, and dialogue in interfaith situations is typical of many branches of modern Judaism as usually conceived in sociological terms. To these may be added the elements of hostility to exclusiveness, assimilation toward the world, and a tendency to withdraw from the private life of the smaller group into the wider social community. Indeed, typical of branch Judaisms is that they do not break away from the Jewish community as much as they break away from traditional Judaism, for they have a disdain for self-definition, and a secret yearning for the dissolution of each and every theologically circumscribed community, for a return to "solitude" in the presence of God. Yet members of the branch burn with such a passion for the present realization of all the currently fashionable ideals of worldliness that they cannot abide the concerns of traditional Jewry.

According to the secular Jew, the further man's knowledge of nature progresses in this age of technology, so that the transcendent interventions of God in Torah receive "natural" explanations, the more completely traditional Jewish faith dies away. Only by means of an extraordinary sacrifice of one's intellect, he claims, by an immolation of one's understanding and reason, is the modern Jew able to cling to a belief in the God of Israel. But as soon as the rationalism of modernity has finally and inevitably become the common property of all Jews, even this final remnant of mythological thinking will vanish.

This is roughly how the situation today appears to the secular Jew, who, of course, can understand the declarations of faith by pious Jews only in the mythological sense. The effectiveness of Jewish faith has always depended quite definitely upon whether, in always involuntarily perceiving things in two different ways, we must have recourse to a sacrifice of our intellect, or whether we can do so with a clear rational consciousness. For faith in Torah Judaism and the God of Israel gives us the strength which we need in everyday life, not when it is sustained by miraculous occurrences and divine interventions breaking through the order of nature and history, but only when one and the same occurrence, an occurrence of which we fully understand the natural causes—for example, the course taken by a disease which leads to a certain death or the fall of a bomb which destroys a house—at the same time in itself appears to us as an act of God, which we receive directly from his hands. But this relationship, which enables us to see two different aspects of one and the same reality is not possible between "contents" but only between two "spaces" in which the same contents are differently ordered. Only thus can we understand the attitude repeatedly adopted by the Israelites of whom the Bible tells.

David has taken to flight after the revolt of Absalom. Shimei curses him and throws stones at him, which is simply a natural resurgence of the old hatred which had arisen through the tribal feud between the house of Saul and the house of David. But David says: "So let him curse, because the Lord hath said unto him, Curse David" (II Sam. 16:10). The calamities which befell Job may similarly be understood as simple natural occurrences: the robbers' raid, the lightning which strikes his flocks during the heavy thunderstorm, and the hurricane which blows from the wilderness and breaks down the walls of the house so that the inhabitants are buried under the ruins. But Job says: "The Lord gave, and the Lord hath taken away; blessed be the name of the Lord" (Job 1:21).

Torah, the secular Jew reminds us, is charged through and through with myth and mythological language occurring in heterogeneous forms. Human history is dominated by a transcendent Creator outside it; atonement to God is made by sacrifice; miracles are performed, and so on. This mythological language is not all of the same kind, and exception may be taken to it, and is, on various grounds. Some of the criticism is familiar and obvious. The basic objection seems to be that myth speaks of the things of God in the language of this world: the acceptance of Judaism as it is "mythologically" presented in Torah puts religious truth into one compartment and scientific and philosophic truth into another—the survival of a "double truth." This mythology is not specifically and essentially Hebraic, the argument runs, but it is the language of a world of the past, now gone forever; to insist on its acceptance is pointless and indeed impossible. The mythological eschatology is discredited because the Messiah has never come. The caveat is entered that Torah mythology is self-contradictory, and that it does not always even succeed in suggesting the spiritual truths it sets out to do. But the chief remonstrance offered to biblical language, and one which shows most clearly the claims for secularizing and demythologizing the Torah, is that myth speaks of God, the transcendent, in terms of an external and objective world, in terms in which it can never be expressed.

This is not the place to raise the pertinent questions of criticism of the Torah's text, but it is important to consider the problem of the justification for speaking of Torah as the Word of God. Traditionally, this has always been seen to be a matter of faith rather than one of text and form. Obviously one cannot regard Torah as the singular and only means by which God reveals himself without maintaining a certain attitude of faith toward the text. By faith Torah is accepted as the canon, or rule, in such a way as to distinguish it from similar literature—Talmudic commentaries, for example—which cannot be claimed as the Word of God. History and criticism can only show that Torah *was* accepted as authoritative, but they cannot prove that one *should* accept Torah. The only alternative to the highly relativistic attitude toward the authority of Torah, to which all purely rational and secular inquiry must lead, is the attitude of faith, which declares that Jews did not make Torah a canon, but that Torah constitutes itself the canon because it has imposed itself as such upon Jews, and invariably does so. Or, in other words, Torah was not at first regarded by Jews as specifically authoritative because it was canonical; it became canonical because it had already made good its authority.

Although problems of authenticity and authority are undoubtedly considered important by secular Jews today, the more essential factor in regarding the Torah canonically has perhaps always been the adequacy and sufficiency of its witness to the revelation of God for the redemption of Israel. As in the Talmud and other major commentaries, so with regard to Torah, the written word suggests what is meant by revelation, but the Word of God is the actual meaning itself. Therefore, for the Jew it is not correct to say that Torah is the Word of God because it makes that claim for itself, nor because the Rabbis have decreed it so in defining the traditional canon. Instead the Word of God communicated in Torah is that which authenticates the written word as *kodesh* ("Holy" Scripture) and gives validity to the canon.

Two misunderstandings of the idea that the Torah is the Word of God are still in wide currency today, both of which are vulnerable to attack by secular Jews on the ground that they enclose the Word in a rigid and static form. The first of these is what may be called an academic view of the nature of Torah revelation, according to which the Word is considered to be revealed and final doctrine—and that includes every point, vowel, and letter of the Bible, the Apocrphya, and the whole of the oral tradition as well, Mekhilta, Talmud, Mishneh Torah, and so on. Rather than being received "separately" as Scripture with historical commentary, the revelation of the oral and written tradition is interpreted as a unitary body of religious doctrines which must be accepted and believed without doubt of reservation. From this point of view the function of Torah is to substantiate the articles of a creed, rather than to convey the Word of God, of which the creed is an exposition.

The second misconception of the Word is that which makes the written Bible fully identical with the Word of God, bringing the doctrine of literal inspiration and "infallibility" to the apex of development. By so narrowing the meaning of the Word that it must be confined to the written tradition alone, some Jews have not only been obliged to distort the literal meaning of the passages of the Bible and mechanize the concept of revelation, but they have violated the Second Commandment by worshiping the book rather than God who utters the Word through the medium of the book. That this form of "idolatry" is widespread in Judaism today—so much so that many antagonists of the Jewish faith, and here I mean secular Jews primarily, think that it is *the* only traditionally "approved" attitude toward Torah—is perhaps easier to explain than its consequences. The craving for objective authority, the sincere belief that faith in Torah Judaism alone and verbal inspiration are synonymous and interdependent, a strong element of conservative sentimentality, and other reasons may be proferred. Basically, however, this "biblicism" is inherent in the type of theology of which it is part. And, as the secular argument runs, instead of serving as a protection for the Torah against the destructive forces of radical criticism, it becomes in itself a virtual foe of Torah by obscuring the relevance of the Word to human experience and by rendering Torah even more vulnerable to hostile criticism.

The reasons which impel most Jews to avoid a discussion of the general conception of reality in a traditional "metaphysical" way have certainly some reasonable justifications. It is said nowadays, for example, that it is not at all the business of Torah Judaism to answer the questions which other Judaisms, on the basis of their own view of nature and reality, put to her. Discussions of this kind, opposing belief and history or belief and science, belong to the period of the older school of apologetics which has now long since been superseded. They can only lead to a new kind of secularism, a "natural theology," and we must not lapse into that. We Jews have no right at all to ask God questions; it is for God to ask questions and to call us to account. These considerations no doubt afford a certain sense of relief for the believing Jew. When he is told this, he has the reassuring feeling that it is no longer necessary for him at all, as a present-day Jew, to concern himself with the fundamental doubts and questions which were a serious stumbling block for earlier generations and which he, too, has already often enough found troublesome.

But these considerations make a completely different impression on the secular Jew, or on non-Jews who are outside Judaism's ambience. The reasons by which Judaism asserts her right to refuse to give any answer to the radical question with which secularism confronts us by the mere fact of its existence do not make upon the secularist the impression of unshakable religious conviction which they are intended to make. Judaism's attitude here tends, rather, to make the outsider suspect that Judaism is perhaps herself not quite certain about the truth of her profession and that this is the reason why she refuses to provide any detailed information about the philosophical basis upon which she stands.

Judaism's future today depends more than ever on whether she withdraws into the ghetto and leaves the world to its fate, or whether she has the authority to continue the discussion with the world outside and to answer the questions which it puts to her. Can we today, even within the milieu of the faith, simply presuppose that Torah Judaism as we have been practicing it is the only way and reject from the outset the overwhelming majority of our contemporaries in their regarding Torah Judaism as an attitude and not as a foundation, as merely a possibility which may perhaps still just keep our heads above water?

At a time when this question is not merely being asked outside the structure of traditional Judaism, but may again arise even in our own hearts, it seems to betray an unhealthy and overtense attitude, a sign of inward uncertainty, if we simply attempt to banish this whole problem to the realm of the subconscious mind. As soon as we raise the question at all, and abandon our violent endeavors to repress it, we can no longer limit the range of our considerations to a single section of reality as a whole—for example, to the account of God's intervention in the history of the Israelite nation. For God is the omnipresent Creator and Lord, who controls the rotations of the galaxies just as he controls the circling of the electrons within the atom.

The attempt to reject out of hand the fundamental question, the question which concerns the whole, does not merely run counter to Judaism's readiness to "come out into the open"; it also brings with it a grave danger for our own personal lives. For in the last analysis it is an effort to overcome the dictates of conscience and a rebellion against God, who has placed us in a reality which inevitably confronts us with questions of this kind and who has given us an intelligence which cannot rest until we have sought for some sort of answer to these questions. The attempt to avoid an honest discussion of these questions may lead to grave consequences at some point in our lives. It may bring about a sudden disaster if these questions arise again under the impact of some great trouble which befalls us.

The secularist obliges us to concern ourselves with a preliminary question, not with the central question of belief. He argues that this preliminary question is a fundamental one, because the entire edifice is in danger of collapse if it remains unanswered. The current dispute, he asserts, in which the "branches" have been engaged loses its relevance from the outset and nothing whatever is to be gained by devoting one's enthusiasm to it so long as no answer has been given to the question whether the whole thing is not, after all, only a projection of human requirements onto the clouds or merely thought-formations which emanate from the individual or collective subconscious of puny human beings.

We can see from all this that, however imperfect and provisional the answer may be which can be given here to the fundamental question with which we are confronted, we must still not repress these questions. We must face them squarely and go into them thoroughly. For what is at stake is the significance and justifiability of all Jewish hope and striving. How are we to set about this investigation? Where are we to start? One begins, I suggest, by permitting the secular Jew to speak his piece; and then on the basis of his report one envisages the conception of reality which is valid according to the larger state of secular research, and to the doctrinal beliefs and practices of traditional Judaism. After that one asks whether belief in a Creator is still compatible with this contemporary secular Jewish view of the universe. In view of this modern world-picture, is it still possible to cling to a belief in a God who speaks through the Torah and intervenes in history? Can belief in Torah be defended against the objections which arise out of the secular conception of the physical universe?

One unfortunate problem is encountered almost immediately. Thankful as we are that at this very time, according to the testimony of leading scientists, natural science has entered a phase which some describe under the heading, "Science on the Road to Religion," we still have from the outset, in dealing with this method of apologetic, the feeling that it brings us into a position of complete dependence upon the momentary phase in which secular research happens to be. We are playing the market, as it were. We are making use of the favorable wind which is coming to us for the moment if not by any means from all Jews at least from some of the acknowledged leaders of secular intellectual thought; we are trimming our sail to catch this wind, so that it may drive the ship forward on her course. But this dependence upon the passing phase of natural science and secular thought in general might immediately become dangerous if the wind were to veer around and if belief were once again compelled to ply to windward.

We need a firm basis which will render us independent of momentary currents of secular opinion. We can attain such a basis only if there is something which lies from the outset outside the whole scope of natural science, some position which is entirely beyond the range of the scientific method, a firm point which cannot be subjected to the spatial and temporal measurements with which natural science works, and which lies even beyond the incalculable dimensions of the universe in comparison with which man sinks into nothingness. We need a position which does not have to be defended against the objections of rationalism, a position from which, if the necessity should arise, we could go over from the defensive to the attack in our relations with secular Judaism and rationalism. Does any such impregnable stronghold exist, which can serve us as a base of operations in undertaking a thoroughgoing settlement of accounts with the presuppositions of secularism in modern Jewish thought? Or is it not true that everything which forms part of reality is drawn, by virtue of that fact alone, into the sphere of secular observation and analysis? That is the question on which everything depends. Only if some such unassailable position exists can we come to grips with the questions with which we are here confronted.